Henry Newton Stevens

Souvenir of excursion to battlefields by the Society of the Fourteenth Connecticut Regiment

And reunion at Antietam, September 1891; with history and reminiscences of battles and campaigns of the regiment

Henry Newton Stevens

Souvenir of excursion to battlefields by the Society of the Fourteenth Connecticut Regiment
And reunion at Antietam, September 1891; with history and reminiscences of battles and campaigns of the regiment

ISBN/EAN: 9783337732431

Printed in Europe, USA, Canada, Australia, Japan

Cover: Foto ©ninafisch / pixelio.de

More available books at **www.hansebooks.com**

SOUVENIR

OF

EXCURSION TO BATTLEFIELDS

BY THE

Society of the Fourteenth Connecticut Regiment

AND

REUNION AT ANTIETAM

SEPTEMBER 1891;

WITH

HISTORY AND REMINISCENCES OF BATTLES AND CAMPAIGNS

OF THE

REGIMENT ON THE FIELDS REVISITED.

By
CHAPLAIN H. S. STEVENS
OF THE REGIMENT.

WASHINGTON:
GIBSON BROS., PRINTERS AND BOOKBINDERS.
1893.

INTRODUCTION.

Only the insistence of comrades whose requests for service I can never decline to comply with could have induced me to undertake the preparation of this volume. It is designed, as believed to be desirable, not only as a souvenir of the trip itself, but to give our guest excursionists explanations and descriptions it was impossible to give them during the trip and to give the comrades historical and reminiscent data and views of places made memorable to them long ago. Should such data not be given now they may never be given.

While the narrative and reminiscent style of writing necessary causes a different treatment of the matter from the purely historical style I have endeavored to *verify* things stated from either personal knowledge, statements of reliable persons or official reports.

In such a work it is neither feasible nor proper that full casualty lists at battles be given nor full mention made of individuals deserving mention.

About securing views of some points desired, especially of our old camp at Falmouth, I have been disappointed, and some views taken necessarily when nature would " weep " have not the clearness wished for ; evoking the confession often necessary heretofore, that with my most thoughtful and strenuous endeavor I cannot achieve all I long to in my work for the regiment.

With unabated affection for the old comrades of the Fourteenth and their friends I submit my work. If it shall please and profit them at all I shall feel recompensed for the care and effort it has caused me.

H. S. STEVENS.

Officers of the
Society of the Fourteenth Connecticut Regiment
1890-'91.

PRESIDENT,	JOHN C. BROATCH.
VICE-PRESIDENTS,	(WILLIAM H. TUBBS. (CHARLES SMITH.
SECRETARY,	JULIUS W. KNOWLTON.
TREASURER,	GEORGE N. BRIGHAM.
CHAPLAIN,	HENRY S. STEVENS.

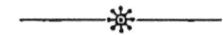

Members of the Excursion Committee.

J. C. BROATCH,	S. A. MOORE,	BENJAMIN HIRST,
G. N. BRIGHAM,	J. W. KNOWLTON,	W. H. TUBBS,
	H. S. STEVENS.	

Officers of the Society for 1891-'93.

PRESIDENT,	A. PARK HAMMOND.
VICE-PRESIDENTS,	(IMRI A. SPENCER, (RUSSELL GLENN.
SECRETARY,	JULIUS W. KNOWLTON.
TREASURER,	GEORGE N. BRIGHAM.
CHAPLAIN,	HENRY S. STEVENS.

The two Round Tops, Gettysburg—from the west.

THE EXCURSION.

WE'RE OFF! three hundred of us, as hopeful, happy, jolly a crowd as one can often see. This fourteenth day of September 1891 marks the consummation of the long-cherished desire of the survivors of the Fourteenth Connecticut Regiment to revisit in a body the scenes of their war experiences and hold a reunion on the battlefield of Antietam, the field where the regiment received its first baptism of fire in the war to save the Union.

Immediately after the battle alluded to there was talk of such a reunion as to be held the next year; but the next year found the regiment just getting well into the war and the next found it still tugging in the harness of war. When the great conflict ended the men all had need to push life's battle of business and support, and they had grown weary of the sight of battlefields and weary of allusions to army life; so it was not until the meetings of a well organized reunion society, held on the anniversary of the Antietam battle, had known a score or more of delightful repetitions that much was said about the long trip and the reunion on the field. Then hearts began to burn and talk to flow. Foremost to suggest and to urge the matter was that comrade supereminently devoted to the interests and honor of the dear old regiment, John C. Broatch. Before the meeting of the society at Guilford in 1889 the president corresponded with railroad managers as to terms and routes. At said meeting comrade Broatch pressed the matter of at once arranging for an excursion, and a committee—comrades Broatch, Knowlton, Brigham, Hirst and Moore—was appointed to consider the matter, with power to act. However, the year was unfavorable and the excursion was not made. At the meeting in 1890 the subject was discussed with renewed fervor, the secretary submitting terms of railroad companies and routes suggested. It was seen to be necessary to act soon if we would make the trip during the lifetime of most of the comrades, and a proposition to make it the next year was unanimously and enthusiastically endorsed by the men at the meeting. Also comrades Tubbs and Stevens were added to the committee. Soon negotiations were entered into with railroad managers for transportation, and circulars were issued detailing plans and calling for enlistments. Chairman Broatch devoted himself ardently to the work of booking excursionists and the other active member of the committee to arranging for the transportation and entertainment of the party.

At first it was thought that if one hundred and twenty-five persons should decide to go the excursion would be a gratifying success, but so popular did it prove that finally more than four hundred were booked.

Many explanatory circulars were issued, numberless letters written, and at last a complete itinerary of the trip was sent to each person on the list; and so thoroughly was the work of preparation done that on the morning of the day appointed for starting all who could go were on hand in time at Jersey City Ferry ready to take the special train of six well appointed cars of the Baltimore and Ohio Railroad Company engaged to take the party out.

The weather that for weeks had been capricious in its temper changed its mood and gave for the start one of the most delicious of autumn days. Of those booked to go many were, at the last moment, unable to leave home or business. Some had dropped out of the list by death. Major J. C. Kinney of Hartford, the first person to forward his name, with that of his wife, for entry, had suddenly been cut down in his strength; and our comrade Priest, whose heart was set upon accompanying his comrades, had as suddenly fallen. Several had, however, applied at the last hour, making of actual excursionists, including those who joined the party at Philadelphia and beyond, not fewer than three hundred and eleven.

And what a company is this occupying these cozy cars as the train pulls out of the station at 1.30 P. M. to move over a portion of the same road the regiment was borne over twenty-nine full years ago! And who can describe the emotions of the veterans as they contrast that day, now so long agone, with this day? Youths they were, most of them, then, leaving home and parents or wives and wee ones for the conjectural hardships and perils of war. Now, men ripe in years, wearing the scars and honors of war and the later honors their confiding fellow citizens have put upon them, they, with their wives, who were then but sweethearts or strangers, their grown sons and daughters and their good neighbors, start on a trip that shall review the scenes of the well-remembered actual hardships and perils of war encountered. Splendid fellows these men were in the bloody field service, and splendid fellows they've proved since in civil life, occupying important places of public trust and in business and social circles; and if only there could be with them this day to share their happiness those other splendid fellows that journeyed with them twenty-nine years ago who later fell on the field by deadly missile or succumbed to disease equally fatal or wasted away in horrid prison-pens or have since the muster-out been enrolled on high, and those disappointed ones who must, perforce, stay at home, their cup would be full. With them, however, are the children of some of our war-slain heroes whose ardor is scarcely less than their own. With them, also, are worthy associates of their own class, comrades Miles, Simmons, Palmer, Higby, Ray, the Davises, Barnes, Hubbard, O'Leary, the Smiths, Gould, Jordan, Condon, Southmayd, Walker, Newton and others of other regiments; also congressmen, state legislators, clergymen, enterprising business men and farmers, and hosts

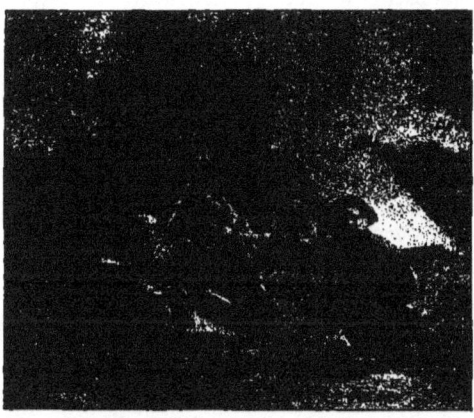

3. "On Picket"—Some of our boys in 1863.

of men and women of finest mold. Was there ever another such party of good, intelligent men and gracious women and bright wholesome youths and maidens as this one now starting with the veteran " boys " of the old Fourteenth on this notable campaign? Scarcely one shows less interest in the primal object of the trip than the veterans themselves. With such a cheerful crowd on such a cheerful day on such a cheerful mission only good cheer could reign. Chatting and chaffing abounded. Old army stories were told and old experiences related. Some of the party found sufficient occupation in observing and discussing the charming scenery along the line of the road, for to most of them this country was entirely new and they had here their first sight of the Alleghanies. Little books of camp songs had been prepared and distributed and soon the strains of " Rally Round the Flag Boys," " Tenting to-night," " Marching through Georgia," " John Brown," etc., told off the fervor of the jubilant crowd and rose above the din of the swiftly moving train. Soon after leaving Jersey City our grand marshal, Chairman Broatch, and our ever genial Secretary Knowlton passed through the train labelling each member of the party for a " Fourteenth man " forever, pinning upon each one the excursion badge. This was the regulation reunion badge of the Society, a plain white badge of heavy satin, having a suitable inscription and the stamp of the Fourteenth—our numeral and initial designation within the old Second Army Corps emblem, the trefoil.

Approaching Philadelphia a brief stop was made to take on recruits, and then the train sped on towards Harrisburg. Large excursion trains over long routes are proverbially behind time and it became apparent that this one was not to go back upon the proverb and that the 7.30 o'clock arrival at Gettysburg assured by the railroad parties was not to materialize. However, there was no discouraging such a good natured company, and there were no terrors to them in the thought of a late arrival; for did they not know that some one was at Gettysburg in advance making full arrangements for their prompt entertainment whenever they should reach there? Many had lunches at hand, and refreshments were brought upon the train, so that none suffered from hunger. As the darkness came on and the train rushed along in a "weird and ghostly way" song and story and chat still abounded. Though a few, with slight weariness, napped enthusiasm increased with most with nearness to their destined goal, the magic word "Gettysburg" thrilling their souls through at every suggestion or thought of it. At last, soon after 10 o'clock, the lights of the old historic town shot out of the gloom and presently the station was reached. Large as was the crowd and mainly strangers in the place, it required but a few minutes to clear station and streets of all. "Fall in for the McClellan"! "Fall in for the Eagle"! "Fall in for Freeman's"! etc., rang out, and soon one hundred and fifty were in line moving towards the first, seventy or eighty towards the second, thirty or forty towards the third, and smaller parties towards other places, following guides; and as soon as they could register and receive the keys of their rooms, already assigned them, and prepare a bit their toilets they hastened to tables laden with tempting food all ready for them. With banqueting and chat and pleasant companionship, the one blessed feature of the whole affair, all weariness vanished. Before midnight nearly all had retired to woo "nature's sweet restorer," for tomorrow was to be a red-letter day to them. Now while they rest and the night is on let us talk of what causes their coming—

THE FOURTEENTH AND THE BATTLE OF GETTYSBURG.

After the battle of Chancellorsville the Fourteenth returned to the old camp near Falmouth, Va., May 6, 1863. Lee, inspired by the results at Chancellorsville and feeling it to be necessary to do something with his army to secure the favor of foreign nations in order to obtain recognition for the "Confederacy" if possible, as well as to keep up the courage and enthusiasm of the southern people, determined upon an aggressive campaign and to take his troops into some northern state.

In May he began the movement of a portion of his army westward from Fredericksburg and then northward towards the Potomac, crossing, soon, one corps into Maryland and moving it steadily towards Harrisburg. As soon as his movement was apparent to the Union commanders some of our forces were moved westward to watch the enemy and be prepared to protect Washington and to give battle whenever necessary or practicable. The troops of the Second Army Corps, to which the Fourteenth belonged, were among the last to leave the southern camps, where for several days we had been under arms before daylight each morning as well as under orders to be ready to march at short notice. That notice came on Sunday, June 14, and at 9 o'clock that evening the Fourteenth broke camp and started northward. On the 26th the Potomac was crossed, and on Wednesday, July 1, when marching through Taneytown, Md., about noon, we were admonished by the sound of guns twelve miles away that a conflict was waging and that probably there would soon be work for all of us. The corps was hurried forward, the sounds and evidences of battle increasing steadily. At nightfall the Fourteenth had reached a point on the Taneytown road near Little

4. Rear of Second Corps position, Gettysburg, Taneytown Road and Meade's Headquarters, seen from National Cemetery.—Round Tops in distance.

Round Top, only two or three miles from Gettysburg, where it was detached from the brigade and sent on picket, not far from the Baltimore pike. The night was clear and bright and to us undisturbed. In all that lovely night there was nothing to indicate the proximity of an armed hostile band or a bloody battle-ground strewn with stark corpses and men anguished with wounds. Nor was there a chance to obtain a true version of the battle just over.

It seems that Lee, finding the Union army following so close upon his course and endangering his communications and likely to at any time bring him to an engagement, recalled his troops that had advanced to York and Harrisburg and ordered them, with those towards Chambersburg, to concentrate near Gettysburg.

On the 30th of June General Buford's cavalry was at Gettysburg, and that night his pickets held a line along a little stream two or three miles west and north of the town.

About 9 o'clock of the next day Hill's advancing infantry attacked this line. The First Corps, General Reynolds, had early that morning started from Emmettsburg, ten miles south, and, hastened by the sounds of battle and the urgent calls of Buford for immediate assistance, Robinson's division

July 1, 1863.

left the main road at the Codori house and crossing the fields and hastening forward was soon confronting the enemy—not a moment too soon. This promptness and the ready acceptance of the gage of battle saved the morning and, presumably, Gettysburg. The rest of the First Corps came up, and soon the ground west and north of the Seminary was one great battlefield. The Eleventh Corps coming up also the line of battle was extended northward to the Harrisburg road. Well, our Union boys did grand battle-work that day, fighting on northern soil, the two small corps being obliged to contend against the rapidly increasing force of the rebels coming in upon all the roads north and west, until finally, fully flanked and overwhelmed by numbers, they were obliged to fall back to and through the town, the victorious hosts following closely, and, coming in upon flank and rear, capturing many prisoners in the streets and narrow by-ways of the town. Fortunately, General Howard had early observed the commanding position of Cemetery Hill south of the town and had sent a brigade to take possession and hold it, and at this barrier the progress of the enemy was stayed. When the Eleventh Corps fell back to Cemetery Hill Wadsworth's division of the First Corps took position on Culp's Hill at its right and the Twelfth Corps, General Slocum, fortified on right of Wadsworth on the other face of Culp's Hill, extending the line beyond Spangler's Spring to Rock Creek; while Robinson's division of the First Corps extended the line on the left of the Eleventh Corps to Ziegler's grove. This was the situation on our front on the night of the first of July. The fighting of our troops that day had been of the highest order. Rarely if ever has it been excelled. Not until nearly all the rebel army was upon them did they yield and fall back. Their pluck that day and the securing of Cemetery Hill in advance made possible our great victory at Gettysburg.

Early on the morning of July 2, the Fourteenth was relieved from picket

5.
Meade's Headquarters, Taneytown Road, 1863.

and ordered to rejoin the brigade. At first the regiment was taken to a field opposite Meade's headquarters on the Taneytown road. About 8 o'clock it was moved across the road, and passing over the wall at the low place below the cottage, seen in cut 14, it advanced up the field and filing right past the barn to the field beyond the barn lane was placed in rear of the brigade on the slope at rear of the Brian premises. The house on said premises, located on the battle-line, was occupied as headquarters by our division commander, General Alexander Hays. Some portions of the brigade that had come upon the ground earlier had gone to the front as skirmishers. At times the First Delaware and Twelfth New Jersey skirmishers advanced several rods beyond the Bliss

6. Meade's Headquarters Barn, and rear of House.—1863.

buildings, one-half mile from the ridge, then fell back to these buildings when pressed. Finally, the line of Union skirmishers was established between these buildings and the Emmettsburg road, the latter passing obliquely along our front some rods in advance of the main Union position. Going upon the ridge we watched with no little curiosity the battle of the skirmishers in front and the work of the sharp-shooters on our crest. The scene on the broad glacis between the hostile lines on that fine summer morning was charming and the work of the sharp-shooters as we watched it grew almost fascinating, we forgetting, nearly, that the game was human. One marksman had made his quarry a wounded skirmisher (one half mile away) unable to stand, who was trying, by a series of flops, to drag his body up the slope to the shelter of his own lines. The marksman fired at him for several minutes as frequently as he could load and take aim; but we confess to a feeling of relief and gladness, and we've felt it ever since when recalling the scene, when the man let up on the poor fellow and had failed to hit him. Truly, war makes game of men, and we all may easily grow reckless in our treatment of human life. And we've always wondered why the comrades of the poor fellow mentioned did not come down to help him off. We doubt that such a scene could have been enacted so close to *our* lines. Indeed, at that very time our ambulances were, in spite of the great risk, venturing out far in our front to pick up our wounded skirmishers. About noon the regiment was moved farther up the slope to Ziegler's grove, then extending clear to the Bryan premises, to support Woodruff's regular battery. About this time occurred, through accident, the first casualty in the regiment; one that put entirely out of the fight one of our oldest officers and came marvelously near ending his days. The horse of a staff officer on the ridge becoming restive and troublesome under the occasional shelling, the officer gave him to a drummer boy to take back to the hollow. The boy mounted, but before he could fully grasp the lines the horse started, and the thumping of the drum the boy carried upon his arm increasing his panic he dashed with headlong speed down the hill. As the boy had control of but one rein his vigorous pulling upon that caused the horse to take a circuitous course, and he made for our regiment. Men rose right and left with all possible celerity to get out of his way. All succeeded except Captain Coit of Co. K, who was just rising and in the act of drawing his sabre when the horse was upon him, striking him full in the face with his breast and hurling him to the ground. The steed was soon captured and taken away, but the mischief he had done did not depart with him. The blow he had given our gallant captain was a serious one, bruising his face and totally closing his eyes for a time. The wonder is that it did not prove fatal, or cause prolonged disability and permanent disfigurement; but in a few days the Captain's handsome face came back to its normal condition, and he was spared for participation in later campaigns and engagements. About this time, also, Adjutant Doten's horse, that nervous, fidgety animal that used to worry Major Clark so, broke away from the boy holding him and dashed down the hill. He was stopped near Meade's headquarters, but when the adjutant went for him Colonel Dahlgren was away with him and had left the adjutant's equipments on his own horse; so the adjutant rode the latter away. He was not grieved at the exchange, as this animal behaved much better on the field than the other. That is how "Old Dahlgren," afterwards ridden by Major Hincks, got into the Fourteenth.

7.   Little Round Top and Round Top at time of Battle.

The regiment was still lying in support of Woodruff's battery, (I, 1st U. S. Arty.) when the attack was made upon the left of the Union line, bringing on the sanguinary conflict of the second day of July. General Sickles had moved out the Third Corps to the line of the Emmettsburg road for a better position, as he judged. Heavy cannonading accompanied the attack, but

SICKLES' FIGHT.

although the Fourteenth was in the track of the shells the configuration of the ground was such that these passed harmlessly overhead. This conflict on the left was one of the fiercest and bloodiest of the war. Longstreet had taken his corps far up to their right, and when Sickles' troops had reached position on the Emmettsburg road ridge he hotly assaulted them at the angle beyond the "Peach Orchard." As soon as one brigade became vigorously engaged another was sent in, and then another, until the weight of the column and the fierceness of the attacks broke Sickles' line at its weak point, the salient, causing it to gradually fall back, after some of the stubbornest fighting ever known. The Fifth Corps was thrown in to help, and the First Division of our corps, in which was the Twenty-seventh Conn. regiment, was sent as reinforcement, losing heavily on the famous "Wheatfield," in front of Little Round Top. Later, the Third Brigade of our division was sent to help Humphreys and sustained a heavy loss. A portion of Hill's corps was put in to aid Longstreet; but night was approaching, the attacking body had lost its momentum and was badly broken up, and our Sixth Corps coming up the action was stayed, our lines on the ridge remaining intact. The time of the commencement of the attack on the second has been variously stated, some lecturers averring that it was as early as 2 o'clock, though official reports of Longstreet's corps demonstrate the incorrectness of this. The writer chanced to be going to the regiment from the hospital barn on the Taneytown road, where he had been with Captain Coit after his hurt, and he took in the ridge on his way. He reached the now famous copse of trees, the so denominated "High Water Mark of the Rebellion," after 2 o'clock and stopped among the guns of Brown's R. I. battery located there. Scanning the field at the left he observed troops moving out and forming

8. Copse of Trees and Round Tops as at time of Battle.

line for some advance, he presumed a reconnoissance in force, and he watched with intense interest the beautiful display as brigade after brigade and division after division moved out and deployed. Officers and their aids in gay dress and trappings dashing here and there and the ranks of men, with bright banners flying and lines of bayonets gleaming, moving with the precision of dress parade made a display entrancing. Far at the left batteries, like vast swarms of moving blackness, were coming out from cover and moving towards positions. When lines were fully formed, the whole corps, known since to have been the Third, moved forward towards the Emmettsburg road. Then the writer penciled in his pocket diary these words: " Corps at left moved out in line of battle about 4 P. M." When the right of the line was hidden in the orchards and shrubbery and the skirmish fire was getting brisk two puffs of smoke suddenly arose beyond our lines at the left. Then the roar of batteries followed, and the commander of Brown's battery sternly called, " Cannoniers, to your posts!" as a cloud of hurtling shells came tumbling in among his guns. The writer at once started for his regiment, running the gauntlet of a fearful shell fire that, with the shrieking and snapping, frightened and bewildered the birds in the air and made them dash wildly in every direction, screaming shrilly—and he penciled right afterward in his

9.
Position of left of 14th C. V. at wall beyond Monument.—Arnold's Battery was at left of road near foreground. "Copse of Trees" and Round Tops visible.

diary: " Cannonading commenced by the rebels about 4½ P. M." That record is conclusive to at least one person. The official report of Col. E. P. Alexander, chief of the rebel artillery, states that he " placed his batteries in *position* about 4 P. M."

Towards evening the Fourteenth was moved to the left about one eighth mile to a stone wall that became its position for the rest of the battle, the wall at which our principal monument stands. It was the extreme left regiment of the division and connected with the right of the 71st Penn. regiment of Webb's brigade of the Second Division of our corps.

At our immediate right was the 1st Del. regiment and at right of that the 12th N. J., and beyond that the 108th N. Y., all of our brigade. In rear of a portion of our brigade was the new (Third) brigade, General Hays' old brigade. At night-fall four men of Co. A. Cooley, Jacobs, French and Geatly, being ordered to go forward to our line of pickets, continued advancing until near the Bliss barn, finding no line, when suddenly there sprang up from the ground several Johnnies and kindly took them in, relieving them of their guns and conducting them to their commanding officer. They were cared for in the well known way of war and booked for a trip—" by hand "—to Dixie. Jacobs, who was something of a wag and a mighty story teller, took pains to enlighten his custodians with amplified accounts of the immense hosts of Pennsylvania militia that were coming in as reinforcements to us. This may account in part for the dismay of some of the rebs. in the attack of the next day when they saw the " Old Blue Club " of our division and found the trained men of our corps ready to meet them and exclaimed : " The Army of the Potomac is here ! "

That evening occurred, not far at our right, the firing and the partially successful attack on East Cemetery Hill by the " Louisiana Tigers " and others, when the First Brigade of our division, Colonel Carroll, was sent from us to assist the Eleventh Corps, coming not back to us during the battle time, though sorely we needed the men on the third. Also, later came the prolonged and desperate struggle of the " Stonewall brigade" and others of Johnson's division to capture Greene's position on Culp's Hill ; followed however by their taking possession, with practically no opposition, of the breastworks at the right of Greene that had been denuded of troops to send to Sickles' assistance. These troops, with four brigades added during the night, occupied all the great space from Greene's position to below Spangler's Spring and pushed their front to the edge of the woods near the Baltimore pike. It required the work of several batteries and the hard fighting of several brigades from 4 to 11 A. M. the next day to drive these intruders out and regain possession of the captured works. The firing of all these engagements seemed very close to the Fourteenth, some of it almost directly in our rear. The early morning firing of the third disturbed somewhat our slumbers on the ridge, but not enough to rouse us thoroughly, for the soldier learns to not trouble himself about what may happen while the picket line remains intact. Rest he needs, and he learns to secure it amid surroundings that might play havoc with a civilian's nerves. When the doughty Captain Arnold, commanding the battery the Fourteenth was supporting, had a brief tilt with a rebel battery, resulting in the blowing up of a caisson on each side and eliciting wild cheers along both lines, we were made thoroughly awake. Then Companies A and F were relieved from picket duty by Companies B and D. The work of these men on the picket line and the relief of the details was quite interesting and exciting to the observers in the rear and looked like a very pretty game—but to the participants it was not pretty. Our picket reserve station was in the Emmettsburg road in front of the regiment. The road was sunken there nearly two feet, affording some protection at the fence. The picket line was at a fence about two hundred yards in advance of the reserve, and the line of rebel pickets about the same distance further on, some of it by the trees at the Bliss orchard. Our men lay flat upon the ground by the fence, hidden and somewhat protected by the posts and lowest rails. Nothing was visible, usually, to fire at, yet when any movement was apparent a shot or two would follow from vigilant watchers ; then the rising rifle-smoke would attract retaliating shots. When the reliefs went to their places there was excitement. The relieving squad would leave the reserve rendezvous moving in any way possible to avoid the observation of the enemy, but when a place was reached where exposure was unavoidable each would take to running at highest speed, and upon reaching the fence would throw himself at once upon the ground. Then must the relieved ones get back to the reserve in a similar manner ; and "relieving" seemed a misnomer. The start of the pickets on either side, to or from their places, was a signal for a lively popping all along the line of their opponents as long as a man was in sight. Not many of the runners were struck, for to hit such a rapidly moving object is a difficult feat; but the pop! pop! crack! crack! would go on all the same ; and the eagerness to hit would make some shooters careless, so furnishing themselves targets for some hidden watchers. Several men were wounded on the line, and Corporal Huxham of Company B was killed. When his squad was relieved he did not stir, and when Sergeants Stroud and Hirst went to him and touched him they found him dead, shot through the head. He was in position, his rifle resting on the fence, his finger on the trigger and his eye apparently glancing along the barrel in aiming. Shot at his post, his face toward the foe and his weapon directed against his enemy—the worthiest eulogy that can be expressed of the soldier.

In front of our skirmish line, a little to the right, eight hundred yards or more from our position at the wall, were two buildings, owned by William Bliss, a farmer. One was a large barn, almost a citadel in itself. It was an expensively and elaborately built structure, as barns go, seventy-five feet long and thirty-three feet wide, its lower story, or basement, ten feet high, constructed of stone, and its upper part, sixteen feet to the eaves, of bricks, the wall being carried to the gables. Within was an oak frame sufficiently heavy for a barn without walls. There was an overhang ten feet wide along the entire front for shelter of cattle, and the rear was banked to the first floor—whence the name "bank barn"—furnishing a drive-way for loads to that floor. There were five doors in the front wall of the basement and three windows in each end ; several long, narrow, vertical slits in the upper story front and two rows of windows in each end. It was a paradise for sharp-shooters with long range rifles. Ninety paces north of it was the mansion, a frame building, two stories in height. As it had a front of three rooms width and two front doors, and there now remain two cellar excavations. with a thick earth wall between, over which it stood, indicating a

THE 12TH N. J. CAPTURES. 17

length of about fifty feet, we see the building must have been long and capacious. On the second of July, when our picket line was established between the Emmettsburg road and these buildings, the rebels settled a force of sharp-shooters in the latter, and the barn proved a veritable tower of

10.
14th C. V. Marker, Centre Bliss Barn site, Gettysburg.—Barn "Bank" in rear.

strength to them but a terror to our batterymen on the ridge, as well as to our pickets on the line, for it allowed a drop-shot upon the latter. Captain Arnold complained that his men were suffering great annoyance and harm from the men in the barn and General Hays ordered its capture. Four companies of the 12th N. J. regiment were detailed for the duty. They charged in gallant style and captured it, with a good number of prisoners, losing several of their own men. With a strange kind of wisdom—from whom emanating we do not know—they soon retired, with their prisoners, to the main line, leaving the barn nicely inviting the Johnnies to come right in again; and soon they were sending their pretty leaden compliments as before. At 7.30 A. M. of the third five other companies of the 12th N. J. again captured the barn, taking two prisoners—and at once repeated the *retiring act*. This sagacious policy of seizing and at once abandoning had its effect, for the returning occupants soon sent the little stingers flying around as before. At last the thing became intolerable. Captain Arnold told the writer that it was such an injury to his men that he asked Colonel Smyth, the brigade commander, if that barn could not be burned. "The enemy would get behind the barn and do us more damage," was the reply. "The walls would be so hot men could not live in them," said the captain. "That is so," replied the colonel. Then an order was issued that the building be captured "to stay," and the Fourteenth, now reduced to about one hundred and twenty men exclusive of those on picket, was ordered to do it. Four companies of the left wing, to be commanded by Capt. S. A. Moore of Co. F, were first detailed for the purpose. Why a force only about one half as large as either of the parties previously sent for the same purpose was sent this time is one of the inscrutable things of the varying wisdom of war. Possibly it was thought that one Fourteenth man was equal to any other two. That it was a serious undertaking all could see, and no man coveted the job—but no choice is allowed the soldier. The detail was taken up towards the division headquarters and then down a lane one hundred and fifty yards to the Emmettsburg road, then across the road, and then into the field beyond, covered for about one hundred and fifty paces by a knoll. When the men came into view of the enemy, now well read in the business and prepared for them, there was a general firing at them from all along the skirmish line and from the host of sharp-shooters in the buildings. Then the desperate character of the sortie was fully revealed, but no man could recoil though death seemed inevitable. As to advance in any kind of a formation would but furnish a better target to aim at, the order was to "go as you please," or scatter and run. Every man was put to his mettle and ran with all his might for the barn. Nearly six hundred yards were to be covered and it was soon accomplished at such speed, but several dropped on the way.

Such was the vim with which the rush was made that the rebs. did not wait to greet their visitors, but "skeedaddled," as we used to say, out of the doors and other openings to take refuge in the orchard and house; the latter, which had not figured much in former attacks, now becoming quite formidable as a place of offense and defense. The little band, quite outnumbered, and beleagured in the barn, could not leave the latter to attack the house because of the marksmen in the orchard and on the picket line, so the remaining four companies on the ridge were ordered to reinforce them and capture the house. Major Ellis commanded this detail, taking with him all except the color-guard. This detail was obliged to move more to the right after passing over the knoll and becoming exposed, and was subjected to a hot fire from the house and skirmish line, and for the last three hundred yards or more to a still hotter one on the right flank that the other had not encountered so fully. A lane, called "Long Lane," narrow and deep, runs out from Gettysburg about one mile to within about three hundred yards of the Bliss house and then turns at right angle up toward the position of the enemy. In this lane had been placed the brigades of Thomas and McGowan to support Rodes in an anticipated attack on Cemetery Hill on the evening of the second, and some say to support the left of Longstreet's assaulting column on the third. When Major Ellis' detail came within about three hundred and fifty yards of the house the whole right of Thomas' brigade began firing, and from them the detail received its worst cutting. Adjutant Doten once referred in a letter to the writer to his emotions in the "rush across that bullet swept plain," and when subsequently his correspondent took him to the Long Lane and

THE PERILS OF THEM.—LITTLE JEFF.

pointed out the location of Thomas' brigade he said at once: "Now I know where that strong flank fire came from!" This flank fire could be termed volleys, and several were hit by it; but the majority, heated and panting, reached the goal, some entering the house and others continuing on to the barn. The men never could describe their feelings on those mad runs for life. We have never heard any really attempt it. The excitement, the frenzied effort, the terrible sense of imminent, savage danger could not be clearly called up nor could words express them—as Lieut. Fiske once wrote us: "When I try to write it I get stuck; in fact a battle is a plaguey poor thing to put on paper—some how it won't *fight*." There fell* on the way Lieut. Seward of Co. I, shot through the body, and Lieut. Seymour, of the same company, shot through the leg. Both got off the field. Little Jeff Brainerd of Co. F while dashing along with break-neck speed fell with a mortal wound. He was the life of his company, full of rollicking fun, and when Capt. Broatch heard him "yell" and saw him leap into the air he thought it was "one of Jeff's antics." Poor, dear boy, when he touched the earth he rose no more unhelped. Sergt. Maj. Hincks as he rushed by heard his shrill cry: "My God! my God, I'm hit!—Oh, how it *hurts* me!" He was borne back and in a few minutes expired while saying to his chaplain, who was holding him and trying to soothe his agonies, "Tell my mother-tel-l-m-y." When the rebels were leaving the house as our men rushed up one of their latest shots gave to Sergt. Baldwin of Co. I a fatal wound, and another gave to John Fox of Co. A a serious wound of the thigh.

11.   The Knowlton Marker on Bliss House site.†   *A. F. Hall.*

The house seemed a poor place for protection, bullets piercing the thin siding and windows, so some of the men left it, running to the barn or taking refuge at the wood-pile or elsewhere out of doors. But it was dangerous exposing head, hand or foot outside of either building, as the enemy had been so reinforced by constant additions from their main line that their guns

---

* No distinctive list of the casualties of the Bliss place affair has ever yet been made. The writer hopes to yet make an approximately correct one.
† This pillar marker was the gift of our Comrade Knowlton.

were ready to cover every point, and the rear of the barn afforded but few openings to fire from. To make matters worse, a battery about five hundred yards in rear of the buildings began firing shells at them, and when their terrific crash was heard the men feared their own doom was sealed. Clements of Co. G was killed by one of these shells, and Lieut. Knowlton received from a scrap "a welt," as he described it, that nearly broke his back. T. W. Gardner of Co. H, while at one of the windows, was struck by a bullet that plowed a permanent furrow along the top of his head.

Though the men plied their rifles the best they could they seemed in a trap and doomed to stay until exterminated, for the order, as understood, was "to take and hold" the buildings. It was not known by them that any modifying order existed, though such had been given. As Col. Smyth was accompanying one detail over the Emmetsburg road Lieut. Seymour went to him and said: "If in event of our capturing the house and barn the rebs. make it so hot we can't hold them shall we fire them?" "We don't know the word can't!" replied Col. S. Hardly had the lieutenant resumed his position at the head of his company when Col. Smyth rode up to him and said: "If they make it too hot for you, burn the buildings and return to the line." No other person than the lieutenant heard the instructions, and when he soon after fell helpless the line rushed on, giving him no chance to communicate the order to the commander—so our men, ignorant of its existence, held on in their beleagured places.

At last those at headquarters seemed to become aware of the desperate straits of our men and Genl. Hays sent them instructions to burn the buildings and return to the main line. The order was borne by Capt. Postles of Col. Smyth's staff, a cavalier true, riding a large, powerful horse. He knew the undertaking was a daring one but he did not understand it fully until he reached a point where he took in at a glance the full line of fire he must run the gauntlet of. Then, as he once told the writer, he said to himself: "My God, there's no chance for me!" But, bold rider that he was, he struck spurs into his horse's flanks, those long, vicious looking rowels we always noticed jingling at his heels when he was on his tours of inspection, knowing that his only chance lay in keeping his horse in swift motion, and dashed on with lightning speed, our men watching in breathless suspense and the rebels holding their guns at sight awaiting a moment's halting or change of direction of the rider to deliver their fire. When he reached the barn, knowing that still he must keep that "devil of a beast" in motion and give the Johnnies no opportunity to draw a bead on him, he made the spurs still do their wicked work, holding with tightest rein his furious charger until the frantic creature leaped wildly into the air, while he shouted his order into the ears of Major Ellis and received the salute of acknowledgment; then, saluting in return, he let out his hand and the horse shot out like a catapult charge and swept away with mighty bounds, the whole skirmish line of the enemy pouring quick volleys after him. His celerity saved him, as it is almost impossible to hit an object moving with such velocity—for when the bullet reaches the point aimed at the object aimed at is not there—

and soon the gallant captain was safe within our lines unhurt, after one of the wildest and most danger-fraught runs ever chronicled. When he reached a point of safety he turned his panting steed facing the enemy and waved his hat to the disappointed "Chivalry"—and they responded with a salvo of cheers.

The order received, preparations were instantly made for firing the buildings. Wisps of hay and straw were soon on fire and by numerous hands applied at different places in the barn, and in the house a straw bed was emptied upon the floor and the match applied. Then the men, taking up tenderly their wounded and dead and gathering their arms, started on their perilous return, running nearly the same hazard as when advancing. When they reached the Emmettsburg road they turned and saw how well they had done their work of destruction, the flames then bursting fiercely out of house and barn. A little halting at the road by a small building in the shade to catch breath and to slake their terrific thirst at a well, and then the boys returned to the ridge to rest and reflect. There have been many strange claims made by men of other regiments to having burned the Bliss buildings, but they have all subsided upon the clear showing of the claim of the Fourteenth, and historians make full concession. Major Ellis made explicit statement of the affair in his official report of the battle written three days after its occurrence, and about five years after the close of the war a large number of affidavits of officers and men of the regiment who participated in it were collected and forwarded to Col. Batchelder, authorized historian of the battle of Gettysburg; and why when in 1884 we were preparing our monument on the ridge we were obliged to contend so strongly to establish our claims against several eager aspirants to the honor surpasses our comprehension.

Purcell's battery of Pegram's battalion that bombarded the buildings claimed that they had fired them with their shells, and one member of that battery once hotly contended with the writer that their claim was well founded and that Genl. Hill had announced it in his official report. It was a simple thing to show him that one hundred men *in* those buildings who were *doing* the firing under stress would be less likely to be mistaken than gunners five hundred yards away, and that two buildings ninety yards apart would not be likely to burst into flames *simultaneously* from shells. Our friend admitted the mistake of himself and his comrades and afterwards explained the modus operandi of his battery. He said the men were directed to place ten shells beside each of the four guns of the battery and to continue firing them leisurely at the buildings until they were vacated. "And," said he, "we fired every one of those forty shells at you." So the men of the Fourteenth who were in those buildings can now gauge the measure of their danger. General Thomas (Confederate) once vehemently asserted to the writer that men of his brigade fired the buildings, but he gave it up; and now we think no ghost of either "Yank" or "Johnnie" will ever rise to dispute the just claim of the Fourteenth.

The daughter of Mr. Bliss writes that when the family returned to their place after the battle most of the wall of the barn was standing, though "all the wood-work was burned out," and that the house was entirely destroyed.

This affair of the Bliss buildings was one of the most thrilling and perilous of the experiences of the Fourteenth. We believe it to have been the most notable episode connected with the doings of any *individual regiment* occurring during the great battle of Gettysburg. It occurred in clear sight of both armies on the wide plain extending between them, eliciting their eager attention and inducing many interchanges of artillery sparring. Had the buildings been destroyed the first time captured by our troops many lives uselessly sacrificed would have been spared and much needless suffering avoided. It was one of the "fool things" of war. Yet it was a grand lesson to our boys, and it furnished one of the brightest points of their most glowing record. In that brilliant sortie some precious lives went out, some cripples were made, and every man that escaped hurt came back panting and wearied and feeling that "out of the jaws of death" had he come.

After the return to the ridge the men lay resting, or preparing their food, or penning notes for the anxious ones at home until the hour of sultriest noon was past. One bit of culinary enterprise, interesting victually if not vitally during this time to several men of one group, deserves chronicling as picturing a bit of soldier life and demonstrating the perfectness of military and moral discipline existing in the Fourteenth. That group gave undivided attention to an endeavor of fire and water to reduce the flesh of a veteran fowl in a pot to an impressionable condition. That fowl a little before was boldly bossing his little company in the barnyard of Mr. Bliss. Sergt. De Forest coveted it, his mouth moist in thought of the delicious fricassees it was evidently created for, but he was too conscientious and too soldierly to lay hands upon it until unquestioned authority was acquired. He approached Adjutant Doten and gravely requested permission to take the fowl under his protection and introduce it (improved) to some of his comrades. The adjutant sympathized with man and bird and thought they should be friends, so he encouraged the alliance; and amid the crack of rifles and the banging of the artillery the sergeant pursued his game until victorious, and he bore it under his arm unharmed to the ridge. When the ball opened later that poultry was still in the pot "kicking" against reduction—and it is still a conundrum with us what became of Al. De Forest's chicken.

While the men were waiting, conjecturing what might be the next move in this gigantic battle-play, well judging it was likely to be a surprise, suddenly it revealed itself. Lee, disappointed that on the first day his army had failed to annihilate the two corps opposed to it and secure a foothold on Cemetery Hill, and still more seriously disappointed at the final almost bootless outcome of the attack upon the Union left on the second as well as the total failure of the attack on East Cemetery Hill on the evening of the same day, and knowing that something more decisive and advantageous must be accomplished by him if possible, resolved upon one supreme effort against our centre on the third. Longstreet, wisely apprehensive of the results of such a movement, advised him that he had still an excellent opportunity to move around the left of Meade's army and maneuver him into an attack; but Lee, put upon his mettle, replied, "pointing his fist at Cemetery Hill, 'The enemy is there and I am going to strike him there!'" He directed Longstreet to take charge of the preparation and execution of the assault,* putting in Pickett's fresh division of his own corps, and promised him troops of three divisions of Hill's corps. Pickett's division of three brigades— Corse's brigade of that division being away south—had not participated at all in the previous engagements, having been left at Chambersburg to destroy railroads. It had come up to within about three miles of Gettysburg by the afternoon of the second and bivouacked there. It was put in motion a little before daylight on the third and by about 7 o'clock was in position, in rear of batteries, one-fourth mile or more to the west of the Emmettsburg road, somewhat southwest of the Codori buildings. At the left of Pickett's three brigades were placed the four brigades of Heth's division of Hill's corps, and at left, or rear, of these two brigades of Pender's division of the same corps, while at the right of Pickett were two brigades of Anderson's division of that corps as a supporting column. It has been put into history that the brigades of Thomas and McGowan lying in Long Lane were designed, and served, as a supporting column at the left, but those officers do not report, officially, as so serving.

There have been various estimates of the strength of the assaulting column, some placing it as high as seventeen or eighteen thousand men. The Confederates, who were wont to announce estimates of their own forces in engagements ridiculously low, give the number variously from eleven thousand to thirteen thousand. Walter Harrison, Inspector General of Pickett's Division, in a published volume from his own hand entitled "Pickett's Men," states that there was in Pickett's three brigades of fifteen regiments that morning "an aggregate effective strength of 4,700 rank and file." There were of the three other divisions furnishing men for the column, omitting the brigades of Thomas and McGowan already referred to, eight brigades, having an aggregate of thirty-five regiments, making with Pickett's men fifty regiments. Some of these latter regiments were larger than those of Pickett's division, but if we estimate their number in the ratio of the regiments of Pickett's brigades as stated by Harrison we have an aggregate force of the fifty regiments of 15,650, which corresponds with General Hancock's estimate given in his official report made soon after the battle that the force "exceeded 15,000 men."

To prepare the way and make effective the onset of this great force Lee directed a cannonading to precede it that he believed might put "hors de

---

*This furnishes reason for calling the assault Longstreet's, though Swallow says it should be called Hill's, as the latter furnished the most men for it. It should not be called Pickett's, as the latter officer commanded only his own division of three brigades, and it never has been shown, so far as we can learn, that he *personally* advanced further than the Codori place, if as far as that, while the other division commanders led their troops until they fell wounded. It should be called Longstreet's charge in order to do justice to *all* the troops of the Second Corps who confronted the array.

combat" our forces on the ridge. Colonel Alexander, chief of his artillery, states that he arranged " 75 guns in what was practically one battery along the Emmettsburg road ridge, disposed to fire at Cemetery Hill and batteries south of it which would have a fire on our advancing infantry," and that there were sixty-three guns at his left along Seminary Ridge (Hill's corps), making an aggregate of one hundred and thirty-eight guns within entirely effective frontal range. There were other guns in their lines beyond, notably the Whitworth, our English friends' present, on Oak Ridge beyond the town that threw several of its bolts into the line of the Fourteenth—in all about one hundred and fifty pieces. The Union position being the inner of the concentric lines afforded less space for placing batteries. General Hunt, chief of our artillery, states that he had "compactly arranged on our left McGilvery's artillery of forty-one guns which with the twenty-six guns of the Second Corps artillery and four guns of Daniel's 'Horse Artillery' aggregated seventy-one guns in position" to reply to the one hundred and thirty-eight guns of the enemy. Rittenhouse's battery of six guns on Little Round Top and eighteen or twenty guns of Osborne's artillery on Cemetery Hill proper could put in some fire, but, as General Hunt says, "they were offset by batteries similarly placed on the flanks of the enemy."

A hush seemed to have fallen on the whole field as the sun passed the meridian and men on either side were listlessly enduring the torrid heat on the unprotected ridges, when suddenly the ball opened and men instinctively knew a Titanic struggle had been initiated. Col. Alexander says: "At exactly one o'clock by my watch the two signal guns were heard in quick succession. In another minute every gun was at work." Our batteries had been directed to withhold their fire in reply a little time until they could locate the most destructive batteries of the enemy and then single out such for special attention, resulting in a more moderate but far more effective fire. The enemy's rapid, hasty firing was not conducive to good aim, as known to us and confessed by them, and a large proportion of the shells passed harmlessly over our line to the depressed ground in the rear, Meade's headquarters building there suf-

12. Meade's Headquarters Gettysburg, after the Battle.

ering severely. When the tornado came our infantrymen hastened to the slight protection of their low stone walls, and soon the mighty chorus was all on. The wall in front of the Fourteenth was a simple affair, but the men crouched down by it as their only friendly shelter. Who can describe their feelings in their helplessness and apprehensiveness during the hour and forty minutes they lay enwrapped in the sulphurous canopy of smoke from our battery near while the awful pounding went on! The palpitating air was filled with the roar of the more than two hundred pieces in incessant discharge, their thunderous explosions threaded and tortured by the screaming, shrill screeching and snapping of the hurtling shells. The rock-based ridge throbbed under the mighty pulsations and the fields trembled with the jarrings of the terrific storm. Closer crowded the men to the wall as the moments, such *long* ones, passed and there was no lull. They heard the cries of the wounded batterymen and the agonized screams of the mangled horses, or the sudden swell-out of the exploding caisson's sound, and all the while in monotonous repetition the orders of the battery commanders near: "No. 1, aim! fire! load!"—"No. 2, aim! fire! load!" the changing voices giving the orders suggesting significantly that some had fallen at their posts. Captain Broatch described it: "The air was filled with smoke so dense that objects could not be seen a distance of four rods. Some shell drove through the wall causing wounds and death. The strain upon the nerves as we lay hugging the ground while fragments of shell were dropping around us was great, and after a while a reaction took place and we dozed, only to be awakened by the bursting of a shell near or the crushing of our stone wall." Sergeant Major Hincks wrote: "One of the guns was directly behind me and at every discharge threw the gravel over me, and I could not only see and smell the thick cloud of burning powder but could *taste* it also. So hot was it that the drops of perspiration falling from my face made mud of the dirty soil on which we were stretched. No one moved or spoke except the gunners behind me." And so these good men lay, in the momentary expectation of being mangled or sent into eternity, never fleeing from their assigned post, enduring horrors of feeling never to be described—all for the Union.

Down upon the picket line and at the reserve post in front our isolated men were in a position as trying between the two fires. Over them was a constantly moving arch of iron missiles screeching like fiends their defiance while passing each other in mid air. Those in the reserve were near enough to the battery line to be exposed to short-dropping shells, one of which fell among them, wounding to the death brave Julian of Co. D. and further wounding Sergt. Hirst and others—but no one dared stir lest a worse fate should befall him. At last the seemingly interminable conflict did end. In about one hour and a half, the Union batteries suddenly ceased action. General Hunt says he ordered this, "seeing the ammunition running low," and it seems also to have been to give the enemy the impression that our line had succumbed and to develop sooner their further purpose.

The enemy's firing continued a few minutes longer and then gradually came to an end. Some of our batteries that were badly damaged or depleted of men were withdrawn and others from the reserve hastened to their places. Arnold's battery, by the Fourteenth, because of its specially exposed position on the highest point of our ridge was used up to a degree surpassing others. The remnants were at once withdrawn.

Now our men breathed again and arose from their constrained positions. Well they knew, however, that a severer, deadlier trial might be awaiting them, but they rejoiced that it might be one they could *face* and give blow for blow in. What Maj. Ellis voiced: " Now they mean to charge with all their infantry!" they anticipated. The battery ordered to fill Arnold's vacated place having, by some misunderstanding of orders, failed to come up the gap must needs be filled by extending still more the slender line of the

13
14 C. V. position by wall in foreground.—Rebel position at trees in background.—Ground over which Heth and Pender charged intermediate.—Orchard far in front shows location of Bliss buildings.

Fourteenth. Maj. Ellis' orders rang out: " Left face! forward, march! halt! front! forward, guide right!" and the boys were in loco permanent. Then, the cloud of smoke having entirely lifted, came a wonderful and startling sight—the emergence of the eleven rebel brigades from cover on the opposite ridge to advance upon us. Pickett's division, having farthest to go, started first, passing through Alexander's batteries and advancing obliquely upon the Second Division of the Second Corps at the clump of trees. Heth's four brigades, commanded by Pettigrew, came over the ridge opposite our division and completed formation on the slope in front. It did not require long to have the whole grand force in array ready to move forward. Pickett's division was arranged with two brigades in front, Kemper's at right and Garnett's on his left, with Armistead in rear of Garnett, the nature of the ground not permitting him to form on the left of the latter. Of Heth's division, Archer's brigade, in the order of the 1st Tenn., 13th Ala., 14th Tenn., 7th Tenn., 5th Ala., was directly in front of the Fourteenth, and at the left of Archer were the other three brigades of the division; while the brigades of Lane and Scales of Pender's division, commanded that day by Trimble, formed in their rear. When all these troops had emerged from the screen of woods on the crest their front reached well down the slope. And what an array! A mile or more in length and several ranks deep of gray uniforms and shining sabres and sabre sheaths, gleaming gun barrels and bayonets, with dancing, showy battle-banners of crimson crossed with starred blue, all glowing under a midsummer's brightest sun! And what an impression of immensity and power those fifteen thousand armed men in alignment gave! It seemed as though they might sweep the continent and trample all things under their feet. Such panoply, moved as to each individual of it by fiery will and resolution and brawny, well trained muscle, might appear well nigh irresistible. To military men the sight was entrancing and an eager desire to watch its fascinating movements the natural one. "'Twere worth ten years of peaceful life, one glance at that array!" But our men knew its significance. The cannons' thunder had been awful and their slanting tornado of bolts terrible, though comparatively harmless, but this array was the lightning, swift, sharp, fierce, aggressive, coming with its multiplied bayonet points straight at their breasts, and they must face it and quench it or woe betide themselves and woe betide the Union they were sacrificing everything to save.

And what was there to meet this? Opposed to the six brigades, twenty-seven regiments, of Heth and Pender were the two brigades, eight regiments, of Hay's division—for Carroll had not returned to us—all these regiments greatly reduced. The Fourteenth had fewer than six score men, and the other regiments of the brigade, though larger, had lost many, while the Third Brigade had lost about one-third of its number in the engagement of the second. At our left there were to confront Pickett and the two brigades of Anderson's division the three brigades of Gibbon's division of our corps, to be assisted by Stannard's "Vermont Brigade." Rebel writers have spoken of the almost imperceptible inclination of the ground in our front as a *steep declivity*, and have mentioned the *several lines* they had to encounter, as "the first line" and "the second line" to drive in and the third "entrenched line" to storm at last, but where our regiment was there was only one attenuated line, and no supports.

Our men at once prepared for the struggle, piling a little the thrown down stones of the wall, emptying their cartridge boxes upon the ground for ready handling of ammunition and resting their rifles on the wall for steady aim; for seconds were precious and every shot must tell.

Instantly upon the formation of lines and throwing out several yards in front a line of skirmishers the enemy began advancing, in a movement so regular, so rhythmical, so automatic in appearance that all seemed some vast, animated machine—and all made straight for the two small, fated divisions of the Second Corps. Pickett moving obliquely upon the Second Division, having the now famous " Clump of trees " as his guide, at first there was a gap between his left and Archer's right, but it lessened constantly, until, when near the Emmettsburg road, in front of the Fourteenth, Garnett and Archer met and lapped. But they were not to come on unmolested, even at long range. Says Alexander: "No sooner had our infantry debouched on the plain than all the enemy's line, which had been nearly silent, broke out again with all its batteries." Lee's Adjt. Genl. says: "As Pickett's brigades approach the enemy's line a most terrific fire of artillery * * * is concentrated upon them." Wilcox, at right of Pickett, says in his official report: "The enemy's artillery opened on them on both flanks and directly in front." Col. Swallow, a staff officer in Ewell's corps, who was, with many other officers, during all the engagement in an elevated position near Gettysburg from which the whole field could be seen without obstruction, says that "when Trimble's column was well out upon the plain artillery suddenly opened upon his lines a most terrific fire from Cemetery Hill, and upon the right Little Round Top was in a perfect blaze and sent forth a continuous and inextinguishable flame of fire, hurling missiles of destruction into our advancing lines." Jones, commanding a brigade in Heth's division, reports: "When about one-half way across the enemy opened on us a most destructive fire of grape and canister." Our Genl. Hunt says: "As the enemy advanced McGilvery opened an oblique, destructive fire reinforced by that of Rittenhouse's six rifle-guns near Round Top which were served with remarkable accuracy, enfilading Pickett's lines." He adds: "The batteries of the Second Corps, having nearly exhausted their supply of ammunition except *canister*, were compelled to withhold until the enemy came within its range." McGilvery makes a similar report, saying also: "We had a raking fire through all their lines. The execution must have been terrible and the effect was plain to be seen." Osborne, whose eighteen or twenty guns were on the southern slope of East Cemetery Hill, reports: "The whole force of our artillery was brought to bear upon this column (the enemy's left), and the havoc produced was truly surprising. We used, according to distance, all descriptions of projectiles." General Howard in official report and in published articles makes similar statements, and the writer's friend of Purcell's battery once told him that after their infantry passed the guns of his battery he walked down the slope about two hundred yards for a better view and he saw "one shell knock out," as it appeared to him, "nearly two rods of men in one rank."

Col. Broatch, in a communication to the writer in 1884, says: "The shells from the batteries away to our left were cutting great gaps in their lines, but they never faltered." Many of our men seem to have scarcely noticed this artillery work, or to have forgotten it, so absorbed were they in observing the formidable force directly in front and in preparing for the coming struggle. Yet that it did occur there is abundant proof, much more than we have adduced. But too great importance has been attached to it as affecting the final repulse of the foe, some even attributing this wholly to it. A writer up of the excursion of the 16th Connecticut in 1890 implies that the artillery did the work of demoralizing and repulsing the charge. Nay, it scarcely affected the ranks except at the flanks. In front of our centre but little havoc was made by it. The ridge opposite the Fourteenth was but about thirteen hundred and fifty yards away. No firing of artillery occurred until the front rank of the enemy was four hundred yards or more down the slope, and the distance to be traversed before the firing must cease because of danger to some of our own positions could not require more than five or six minutes for a quickly marching column. But a few hundreds could be knocked out in that time, and even if a full thousand had been what would they be out of over fifteen thousand? The firing shattered the lines at the ends only, and these lines steadily closed up and pressed towards the centre, keeping that intact and solid all the time. Our men saw but an undiminished, really increasing, array of a vast, moving hostile force, and knew that upon our infantry depended its defeat.

As the rebel pickets on the line fell in with the advancing skirmishers our skirmishers on the front line rose and slowly fell back, firing into the faces of the foe. When the order was heard: "Rally on the reserve!" they joined the latter and all fell back to the position on the ridge, taking their places among their comrades—and now all the members of the little Fourteenth band were together, shoulder to shoulder ready for the supreme, crucial moment, with tingling nerves and bated breath awaiting the onset. Hardly could they be restrained from firing when the enemy came near enough for their good rifles to reach them, but the strict order of General Hays had been announced that not a gun should be fired until the enemy should reach the Emmettsburg road. Major Ellis emphasized this order, Adjutant Doten went forth and back along the line repeating it, and Sergeant Major Hincks and the line officers reiterated it--and so our men, with aim well taken and finger on trigger, submissively waited. The long range batteries had nearly all ceased their firing and a stillness supervened that made the sound of the enemy's tread audible and the calm orders of the officers: "Steady men! Guide centre!" to come up as distinctly as though delivered on dress-parade.

Just after Archer's line and Garnett's lapped and the men of Virginia grasped the hands of the Tennesseeans the fence was reached, and simultaneously with it rang out at our brigade the order: "Fire!" "Fire!!" "Fire!!!"—and our rifles spoke in a volley so full, so well directed that the front line of the enemy mounting the fence seemed wiped away.

Swallow, who was intently watching, says: "As soon as the top of the fence was lined with troops the whole line tumbled over, falling into the bed of the road, while the enemies' bullets buried themselves into the bodies of the falling victims. * * * Scores of survivors often related their anxious suspense and the length of time it seemed to climb to the top of that fence." Yet hundreds pressed over, forming a strong array to advance against our position, and Garnett's men to attack the angle close at our left. No battery helped our end of the division for the one ordered to replace Arnold's had not yet come up, and our men must rely on their own pieces alone. Their nerves were steady, their courage was grand, and they plied their weapons with such swift, remorseless stroke that the enemy went down like grain before the reapers. That tempest of lead they could not hold against. As Longstreet said: " When the line behind that stone wall rose and delivered its fire mortal flesh could not withstand it." But their pluck is good and numbers attempt to drive on, judging it impossible to retreat; until shattered under the pitiless storm, their hope gone, they fling themselves upon the ground or take shelter behind any possible object. Trimble's two brigades in second line have struck heavily the right of our division but have been completely repulsed and broken up by our unflinching infantry, assisted by Woodruff's guns well served with canister.* Kemper at right of Garnett, deflected to the right by the Codori buildings, turns by half wheel to left to

14.
Codori Buildings and ground over which Pickett's Div. advanced. Lone Tree at extreme right of middle ground is at corner of Angle where Cushing's right gun stood. Right of Wall was left of 14th C. V.

strike the brigades of Hall and Harrow of the Second Division and the left of Webb at the clump of trees, but McGilvery's guns and Stannard's muskets smash his flank and Hall and Harrow break him all up. And now the vital moment of the great battle has come. Armistead, who, shielded by Garnett, has received but little harm, crossing the Emmettsburg road forms rapidly his men for a charge, and dashes, at the double quick, the double and tripple-shotted guns of Cushing flinging canister into their faces, against the

---

* Major Hincks wrote: " All semblance of lines cease and what had advanced as an army began to fall back as a mob—not all along nor rapidly, however. They still turned and fired and now and then made a brief stand."

The Climax.

angle.* In a few moments his men are there, and some have swarmed over the wall and seized some guns, one color-bearer leaping upon the gun nearest the Fourteenth and waving jubilantly and defiantly his flag. The moment is a critical one. If the mass passes through and the point is held what can we say for the army and what for the country? Major Ellis sees the situation; quickly he decides. Out rings his order: " Fourteenth! left oblique. fire!" and the hundred rifles play quickly their hot volleys into flank and front of the surging host. the First Delaware on our right doing the same: and quickly as a spasm the fray is over. Armistead had leaped the wall with fifty or sixty of his men and advanced a few paces within the angle, but it availed him nothing, for in a few moments all, leader and followers, were stretched upon the ground lifeless or wounded or were made prisoners. This last, desperate struggle that might seem long was but brief. To our men it seemed a wild, swift, bewildering dream of a few minutes—rush, crash, turmoil, slaughter, dissolution. Our friend of Purcell's battery, who was watching it with eager solicitude, says he saw an officer (Armistead) "holding up something on a stick or sword," lead his men on a rapid charge against the wall; that there was a boiling commotion, a fierce struggle, and then all was over—" all in a few seconds." Pickett's Inspector General says: "Our men swarmed over the fence and among the enemy's guns and were swallowed up in smoke—and that was the last of them."†

The scene now in front of the Fourteenth was indescribable. Poor wounded wretches, scattered or lying in heaps, over the fields and in the road far in front, were writhing in agonies or straightening out in the last death shiver. Some unhurt ones who dared were running with all their might to reach their own lines. Some of Armistead's men, pressed out beyond the angle in front of our men, were daringly grouping for some resistance, or flinging themselves upon the ground with Pettigrew's men, while a sizable group still clung to the front of the angle for protection and maintained their firing. Those upon the ground, now thoroughly bereft of hope and filled with fear, raised handkerchiefs,‡ that looked like leaflets fluttering in the breeze, and waved them above their heads, crying out mightily for quarter. By the

---

*Note.—When standing near our monument at G. a few years ago Captain Doten pointed to the spot, about two hundred and fifty yards at front and left of us, where he saw a mounted officer (Armistead undoubtedly) form his brigade, on the run, in column of division and without a moment's interruption charge at the angle.

†The same authority says of his division: "On the morning of the 4th we could not report an aggregate of 1,000 muskets, and this after returning to the ranks and arming all the cooks and ambulance men." He further says: "The exact number of the killed, wounded and missing as subsequently ascertained amounted to 3,393; just about three-fourths of the force carried into action." Reports of Heth's and Pender's officers show losses in nearly the same proportion. Archer's brigade, in front of the Fourteenth, lost more than one-half of its men its commander reports, and he adds: "Of the seven field officers who went into the charge only two came out." Our boys took in some of them.

‡Of these handkerchiefs Maj. Hincks wrote: "Where they got them all I don't see, for upon a closer view afterwards we failed to see anything white in either their clothing or complexions."

time of Armistead's charge the men of the Fourteenth had become so excited that all precautions to keep sheltered were set at naught, and they rose, wildly cheering and shouting and firing as rapidly as possible. Because of this several were wounded who otherwise might not have been, Lieut. Tibbitts for one, and brave Goodell was killed. But exultation had begun to swell their breasts and would not be suppressed, and in memory of past disadvantages this one great opportunity called out shouts: "Give it to 'em boys!" "Now we've got you!" "Sock it to the blamed rebels!" "Fredericksburg on the other leg!" "Hurrah! never mind who's hit, give it to 'em!" —and many another phrase not current in these lines. When the total collapse in front came the spirit of the men was unrestrainable. They ran down from the wall gathering in their tale of prisoners and seizing battle-flags. More than two hundred men, field officers, line officers and men of the ranks, were captured by our jubilant boys; and the same scene was enacting all along the front of our division. One flag was flying defiantly directly in front of the regiment's centre, about ninety yards away. Maj. Ellis called for volunteers to bring it in. Capt. Broatch leaped the wall, calling: "Company A, rally for that color!" Lieut. Brigham also started, eager to secure the prize, but quickly fell with a foot wound that crippled him for life. Sergt. Maj. Hincks, who had already made up his mind that he *must* have that flag, started; and running straight towards it our slender limbed Mercury outstripped all competitors and, regardless of thickly flying bullets from foe and friend, and unharmed by them, reached and seized the " banner with the strange device " and bore it back, amid the cheers and congratulations of his comrades. It was the flag of the 14th Tennessee and was the first color captured. Brave Corpl. Chris. Flynn of Co. K rushed down, heedless of dangers, and snatched the flag of the 52d North Carolina from its guard, and E. W. Bacon of Co. F, with equally perilous run, seized that of the 16th North Carolina.* Those of the 1st Tennessee and 4th Virginia † were captured by others.

While our commander reported *five* battle-flags captured by the regiment there has been a general belief among our men that *six* were taken. The diary of Sergt. Wade of Co. F reads, " We captured 6 battle-flags," and in the diary of the writer appears, as penciled that eventful evening: " The regt. took more than 200 prisoners and 6 colors." Others made similar notings. Perhaps the matter is explained in the statement of Frank Somers of the band that " one flag captured, a splendid silk flag, was torn off the staff by the finder and concealed under his coat until he got a chance to send it home." This may have been the missing sixth.

---

* Messrs. Hincks, Bacon and Flynn afterwards received the United States Medal of Honor for deeds of special bravery.

† There must be a mistake as to the capture of the color of the *4th* Va. though so reported by Maj. Ellis. The 4th Va. was in the old " Stonewall Brigade " in Ewell's Corps and was at Lee's left engaged against Culp's Hill. The *14th* Va. was in Armistead's brigade, a part of which was opposed to our regiment, and presumably it was the flag of that regiment instead of that of the *4th* Va. that was captured.

When the enemy was well broken up in our front a battery of brass guns, long delayed. came up to replace Arnold's. One gun was quickly wheeled into position near our left, loaded with canister and fired at the retreating ones. The result was, that one of our regiment was killed and others hurt. Henry Hasler of Co. K, who was just in front of the gun as about to be discharged, saw his danger and flung himself upon the ground just in time to save himself; and his remonstrances, with those of others, prevented any further use of the piece there.

Well might the Fourteenth rejoice at such success at their position. They had the weakest line, as to numbers, along the front, and when the repulse of the enemy was accomplished scarcely a cartridge remained in the regiment. While the right of the brigade was supported by the Third Brigade and helped by Woodruff's battery our regiment had absolutely no supports behind its single thin line, and had the attacking force maintained its alignment a little longer and been able to push on a little farther one cannot tell what the consequences might have been, for our men could then have met them only with clubbed muskets.

One incident shows the significance of their work. As our prisoners were being conducted through our line one sturdy fellow, glancing along our position and exhibiting surprise, inquired: "Where are your men?" "Here they are," was the reply. "I mean those you had here that gave us such volleys as we advanced," said he. When assured that all we had at first were still there except the disabled, he exclaimed: "We could have gone through if we'd had another line of men!" Then taking another look he said, with stronger emphasis: "My God, we could have gone through as it was if we'd known how few you were!" Then he muttered, with an oath, as he passed over the ridge: "I'd like to try that over again!"

It is true that one division of the Twelfth Corps had been sent by Genl. Slocum, as he reports, "to reinforce the centre" if the enemy should drive our line from its position, and Col. McDougal, commanding a brigade of this division, reports: "I proceeded with my command to the rear of the left centre, near the headquarters of the Commander in Chief." Col. Wooster, commanding the 20th Connecticut in the latter brigade reports: "The regiment, with the remainder of the First Brigade was then moved across the Gettysburg (Taneytown) road to support the centre in an attack then being made." Comrades of this regiment show that they were located in the vicinity of the barn on the Meade's headquarters place. These reinforcements all returned to their old positions unused. Our line was not driven, and the great victory of the day, the greatest of the war, when, as all confess, the "backbone of the rebellion was broken," remained with the glorious old Second Corps, and no insignificant part of it with the regiment whose doings our lines are chronicling.

Well, we paid dearly for it. In all, sixty-six out of about one hundred and sixty had been lost to us. Thirteen were killed or mortally wounded, forty-nine wounded and four captured. Some of our wounded received three or four hits. Right upon the close of the action, among other expressions of exuberant rejoicing Genl. Hays came cantering by, sans coat, sans hat, sans collar, his shirt loosened at the throat, holding in each hand a rebel battle-flag which he was trailing upon the ground amid the cheers of our exultant troops. The evening was a glad one to us. The Fourteenth was never so happy before. Small as it was, as said the little gleeful darkey when asked how old he was: "Well, if you goes by what marm says I spose Ise about ten yees old, but if you reckons by the fun Ise had I guess Ise about a hunder," so our boys could have said, in numbers we are about a hundred but in feelings we are about a thousand. They waited the dark night through, largely sleepless however, apprehensive that the enemy might attempt another sortie.

15.
Hays' Headquarters after the Battle.—On the battle-line 3d Div., 2d A. C.

Right here we must allude to the almost utter failure of some of our men to recall the action and noise of the artillery during the final struggle, even of Cushing's and Woodruff's batteries so near. Of the cannon work at our right Capt. Hazard, in command of the Second Corps artillery, reports: "Woodruff still remained in the grove (Ziegler's) and poured death and destruction into the rebel lines." Lieut. Col. Bull of the 126th N. Y. regiment, commanding our "Third Brigade," reports: "The enemy * * were subjected to a murderous fire of musketry and artillery;" and in a history of the 126th N. Y. it is stated that details of that regiment helped serve the battery guns during the last effort.

Scales, commanding one of Pender's brigades, says: "The brigade encountered a most terrific fire of grape and shell on our flank" (from Osborne), "and grape and musketry in front." Lawrence, commanding the 34th N. C. regiment, and others report similarly. As to Cushing, General Webb says, in official report: "Three of Cushing's guns were run down to the fence carrying with them their canister." General Gibbon says: "Our guns were then well forward * * loaded with canister. * * * As the front line came up it was met with a withering fire of canister and

HELPFUL BATTERIES—CUSHING'S DEATH.

musketry." A line once received from our Broatch reads: " The enemy captured three guns at the projecting angle of the wall at our left which had been advanced from one of our batteries." Comrade Henry Hasler, of Co. K, once sent the writer some of his reminiscences of the fight. Accompanying the writing was a diagram of the battle-line of our two divisions, singularly accurate for one drawn from memory after so many years, showing Cushing's full battery located at the front fence in the angle. But the best testimony, and irrefragable, is from a letter in the writer's possession written by Lieutenant (now Captain) Frederick Fuger of the 4th U. S. Artillery, who was Cushing's sergeant at the time of the battle. It is interesting as throwing light upon the doings of the battery and as giving the true version of the death of Lieutenant Cushing; a death invested with false. legendary glamour, the legend perpetuated by the published repetition of General Doubleday and extensively quoted from him. Fuger writes: " On the morning of July 3, 1863, Battery A (Cushing's) occupied a position with their six guns about 150 feet from the stone wall which was directly in front, and we kept that position until the artillery duel ceased on both sides. After the firing ceased General Webb came up to where Cushing stood and said to Cushing, ' it is my opinion that the rebels will advance their infantry and attack our position in force.' Cushing replied, ' then I had better run my guns right up to the stone fence and bring up all the canister alongside of each piece.' To which Gen. Webb said, ' do so.' The command was immediately given and the six guns were run by hand to the stone fence, leaving just room enough between the wall and wheels for cannoneers Nos. one and two to load ; limbers and caissons did not move. At this time Lieut. Cushing was not wounded. Within fifteen or twenty minutes after we had our guns in the new position the rebel infantry were seen advancing. The 72d Pa. were directly in our front on the skirmish line and were obliged to fall back as the enemy advanced in force. As soon as our battery was unmasked by the 72d P. V. and the enemy were within 400 yards of us we commenced firing single charges of canister. and at about that time Lieut. Cushing was wounded in the right shoulder. (Gen. Webb says the right shoulder-strap was shot completely off yet not wounding him.) When the enemy came within 200 yards we fired double charges of canister with terrible effect. Cushing about this time was again wounded in the scrotum, but still he stuck to his post and would not leave the battery. All this time I was right alongside of Cushing and imparted his orders to the men. Still the enemy advanced and Cushing ordered the men to triple the charges in the guns. While finishing the command he was shot through the mouth and instantly killed. At this time he was about one yard from the trail handspike, and to the right of it, it being No. 3 piece of the battery. I stood to his right, about two feet from him, with my pistol in my right hand. When I saw the lieutenant fall forward I dropped my pistol and caught him around the body with both arms. I saw that he was dead, and ordered Wright, of the battery, to carry Cushing's body to the rear. Lieut. Neilm * * * who had command of the left half of our battery, was killed just a moment before Cushing, which left me in command. The insinuation of history that but one gun was run down to the wall is wrong. The report that Lieut. Cushing's bowels were shot out is all nonsense. Again, Lieut. Cushing never fired a gun; there was no occasion for him to do so. We had enough men left to do that. The Lieutenant had enough to do to watch the enemy and give the necessary commands. After sending Cushing's body to the rear I fired a few rounds of canister; when the enemy was almost on top of us I ceased firing and told the men to pitch in with anything they had in their hands, such as pistols, sabres, sponge-staves, and handspikes, which I am glad to say they did in good style. * * * A few minutes and all was over, the rebels retreating. The wall was about fourteen inches in thickness and the muzzles projected over it."

Of the writer of the above valuable contribution to the *exact* things of the battle Genl. Hancock says in his official report: "I desire to bring particularly to the notice of the Major General commanding the case of First Sergeant Frederick Fuger, Batty. A, 4th U. S Arty. During the action of the 3rd his conduct was such as to entitle him to promotion, and his character is such as to make this a proper method of rewarding his services." That any of our men should have seemed unconscious of the work of Cushing's and Woodruff's batteries at this stage of the action, or that impressions made on their minds should have been instantly effaced, is not surprising. so intensely absorbed were they in their own thrilling danger and with the demand upon them for desperate action—as even in our quiet home we have, at times, been so absorbed in writing or reading as to be oblivious to terrific thunder-storms that have frightened all others in the house.

On the morning of the fourth the rebels advanced somewhat their picket line and manned it strongly, to keep up the show of force, while all the time the troops were "silently stealing away." Our regimental dead were buried on the ridge, near our position. "The graves of five corporals stand in a row, all neatly marked with the name, date and regiment," records Major Hincks. That day our men went into the fields in front, though savagely fired on by the hostile pickets, to bring in the suffering rebel wounded lying there in hundreds, moaning or shrieking in their pain—as indeed we had heard them all through the night previous. Our surgeons and hospital force were entirely occupied night and day with the care of the thousands or wounded of both armies needing immediate attention. It rained heavily that day, increasing our difficulties. On the fifth, Sunday, it was evident that Lee had retreated. Details were sent out to collect abandoned arms. and other details to bury the masses of the rebel dead—a sad, sad job. They found the dead in some places so numerous that the ground appeared covered by them, and one could walk for distances stepping only on bodies of the slain. The Emmettsburg road directly in our front seemed packed with them—vast hecatombs to the insatiate Moloch of the cruel and causeless slaveholders' rebellion. The sight of some of the dead was moving to the sternest hearts. Some were in attitudes indicating that life went out in agony, and others holding likenesses of home loved ones they had spent their last moments in gazing upon, or staring with glazed eyes upon the blessed scriptures that had solaced the dark hours when " all *men* had forsaken them." One not yet dead, a mere lad, lying on the wet muddy ground, groaning and writhing in his physical torture, when inquired of as to his suffering replied, as says Sergeant Wade: " Dreadfully! dreadfully! O that my mother was here!" Was he very unlike our own " Little Jeff?" That afternoon the regiment left the ridge and moved to a locality called Two Taverns, on the Baltimore pike, and on Tuesday, the seventh, joined the advancing movement of the corps in pursuit of Lee.

Much stress is laid by Confederate writers generally on an asserted great numerical disparity between the forces of the two armies engaged, some extravagantly saying that Meade's army outnumbered Lee's as two to one. To say nothing of the demonstrated fact that the average Union soldier was equal in battle-work to the average Confederate, we think him proved to have been a little better, careful computations place the number of combatants present as in the ratio of about seven to six or eight to seven in favor of the Union army, but in many other respects the advantage was greatly with Lee. His men had been marching quite leisurely, living in a land of plenty, and were in the best of condition. In each separate engagement of the three successive days the Confederates were the attacking party and in each instance greatly outnumbered their immediate opponents. In such instances unless the attacked force is strongly entrenched the advantage is usually with the party making the attack, and it was markedly so at Gettysburg. Lee would mass, unobserved, a great force against some point of our line and our leaders would not dare, in the uncertainty, to weaken any other portion of the line to strengthen the point of possible danger. On the first day about two-thirds of Lee's army had, before evening, fallen upon our two small corps* well exhausted. In each of the attacks of the second and third of July he had prepared an immense column and had launched it upon us suddenly. If anyone asks what gave us the victory at Gettysburg we unhesitatingly reply, the stern, unflinching courage of our men and the signal unity of purpose and thorough devotion of our commanders. Said to the writer one blood-covered man just out of the vortex of flame and death at the left on the second: " I never knew our men to fight as they do to-day—they cannot be whipped." The words of Goodell of the Fourteenth, who, brave fellow, fell dead, his head pierced by a musket ball, soon after uttering them: " I would rather be killed than beaten to-day!" expressed the common sentiment of our men.

And now, though we have not related a moiety of what we might upon our subject, that which has induced our large excursion, we must cease our talk, for the night is spent and our " boys " and excursionists are awaking —that is, such as have slept at all, for the memories of Gettysburg were so hot within them that sleep was barred out with many—and early on this

---

* The Confederate corps, divisions and brigades were much larger than the aggregations of corresponding designations of the Union army.

fragrant morning moving squads of them are already out threading the quiet streets on their way to the sacred old stone wall to feast their longing eyes on a view that memory has kept constantly with them these twenty-eight years. And the others are astir soon, young men and young women, awake to the great sentiment and history of the place, and the wives and friends of the vets. who have heard for almost a lifetime of Gettysburg and what the Fourteenth did here, are out noting the features of this quiet old town and preparing for jaunts over the field. The curious old public square, unlike anything seen in New England; streets intersecting the Baltimore pike, here called Baltimore Street, one of the most interesting streets in our country's history, all lined with smallish, stoutly built, snug old houses of plainest architecture; buildings of note, as the one whose steeple Genl. Howard used as a watch-tower, others that had some of the shells of the battle protruding from their walls, all attracted their eager eyes, and they thought of the day when our men were hurrying adown these ways, many of them to be shot down or captured by the crowding hosts of the exulting enemy. And they thought, too, of the hours when Lee's troops held these streets and houses and filled the square with their batteries or cavalry, expectant of soon " wiping out the Yankees;" and then of the day when this same boastful host, after receiving its most crushing, mortifying defeat, had silently betaken itself away, bearing disappointment, wounds, heavy losses and forebodings.

Breakfast in due time ready and disposed of, by 8 o'clock carriages began to arrive for battlefield parties. A large array of them gathered at the McClellan, with Capt. Long as guide; another large array at the Eagle with Mr. Minnich as guide; while other smaller groups were ready with services at lower rates for such as wanted them. The carriages did not need to wait long for their patrons, and in short space the gay, eager crowds were on their way to what they had long been craving a sight of, the battle-lines and battle-fields of Gettysburg. Many of our boys preferred to do the fields on foot, especially as enough had been there before to serve as guides for others, and so started in little squads, discussing the battle and the place and repeating reminiscences all the way as their footsteps kept time to the beating of their well roused hearts. Some parties went to East Cemetery Hill, to have indicated to them upon the wonderful panoramic display before their eyes the place at the little hamlet of Cashtown among the mountains whence Hill's corps, on the morning of the first of July 1863, advanced to strike Buford's cavalry; the points where the other rebel troops came in from the directions of Harrisburg and York and almost surrounded the troops of the First and Eleventh Corps, driving them, after hours of brave and stubborn resistance, upon and through the town and upon this very hill; the place of the severe cavalry engagement of the third day in the distance; Culp's Hill at the right, on whose visible front, not far off, Wadsworth entrenched on the night of the first day, and on whose other front Greene's brigade of the Twelfth Corps completely foiled five fierce onslaughts of some of Early's brigades; the noted ground at their feet where the " Louisiana Tigers " and others made their wild dash, getting among the guns of Rickett's and Wiedrich's batteries,

16. Group 14th C. V. Excursionists on East Cemetery Hill, Gettysburg, September 15, 1891.

whose locations are now indicated by actual mounted guns and lunettes ; and the famous cemetery close by, where Howard had his headquarters and which he held in spite of determined assaults. Then they went to Culp's Hill to view the ground of the desperate charges of Stewart and others to capture Greene's position ; then along the line where the enemy succeeded in entering and occupying, in the absence of troops once holding there but sent that afternoon to reinforce our left, a most promising location between portions of our forces, viewing the fine monument of the 20th Conn. on this line; then to Spangler's Spring, a lovely woodland spot, where (and this is no myth) Yank and Johnny met late at night of the engagement of the second and conversed, all unconscious at first that they were not all " of the same faith." Of course the ubiquitous photographer* had followed and a group picture was taken on Cemetery Hill.

17. Spangler's Spring, Gettysburg.

After a dinner hearty enough for giants and seasoned with war appetites, all parties started out again. Some went over the first day's field, surprised that it proved so interesting and that the battle there was so extensive and protracted, with so many features of severe encounter. Parties to Little Round Top were treated to a view showing a large part of the battlefield from far below where Hood's men rendezvoused to far above Gettysburg, and the guides and lecturers pointed out the positions of the engagement of the second day ; the " Wheatfield," right under the eyes, looking to the front, where wondrous slaughter was, ground that on that battle morning was " a beautiful field of uncut wheat and at night it was hard to tell the growth ; " Trostle's farm, the scene of dreadful carnage : Houck's Ridge, where men battled

---

* In the party were three kodakists. Messrs. Hall, Hammond, and Blatchley, and one photographer, Dr. Sweet.

like tigers and left the rocks and earth gory; the " Peach Orchard," famed evermore for its bloodiest of fighting, and wild " Devil's Den," the natural stronghold of sharpshooters, close under to the left. Northward, on the right, could be seen all the Union position to East Cemetery Hill, and opposite that Seminary Ridge, the location of Hill's corps, to its termination beyond the town; and beyond that Oak Ridge. Down to Devil's Den the group went and felt no surprise that the wild, disordered mass of rocks had received such a sulphurous name nor that the rebel cracksmen found it so fine a place to gather, for a time, a harvest of our choicest ones on the hill; and they did not regret to be told that when our marksmen got in their work from the sides of leafy Round Top they mercilessly " cleaned out " the pestiferous nest of destroyers. On the way, one large party, desirous of seeing and standing on the Bliss place, and finding it a feasible thing,

18. Some Rocks at Devil's Den, south side.

left the conveyances in the Emmettsburg road opposite the main position of the Fourteenth and crossed the fields one-fourth mile or so to the premises. There was emotion not easily expressed when they stood on the veritable ground of the thrilling adventure, by the marker on the barn site.* Mr. Bunce and other steadfast old friends of the regiment who had heard much about it were as interested as the " boys," and listened with rapt attention as comrade Broatch detailed the movements of the charge and pointed out the places, all visible to the listeners, and described the scenes in the barn and house, and as Chaplain S. detailed additional features of the affair and gave description of Capt. Postle's ride and the story of the rebel batteryman. Sergt. Hyde

---

* The Regtl. Soc. owns, by purchase, one acre of the Bliss place ground including sites of the barn and house. It gave permission to the 12th N. J. to erect a suitable marker there.

added some of his own recollections of the affair as he saw it from the skirmish line. While at the wall near the large monument comrade Broatch gave a graphic description of the charge against that very position on the third of July as seen by the Fourteenth men engaged there. The guide-lecturer standing by took mental notes, for this talk from one who was there and saw it all and was a participant in the struggle and could relate it so intelligently went beyond anything he could do.

Mouth of Devil's Den, Gettysburg.

That evening though, the body of each was weary no one's spirit flagged, and to keep still was impossible. Enthusiasm of old comrades, meeting at such a place and time, after years of separation since they trod in company war's harshest path, could not be restricted to a few hours. Through the thoughtfulness of comrade Coit and others a local band had been engaged to play in front of the McClellan, to the delectation of some of the people, even if Gilmore had dropped out of it and none of the "Marine Band" graduates were in it. A delegation of about eighty of the 108th N. Y. regiment, of our old brigade, just in on a train, came up to fraternize with their old associates, and speeches, renewing old friendship and recounting old adventures, were in order.

The next morning, September 16, all were out in right good season, bright and breezy and with appetites for adventure whetted by the former day's trips, for their last touch of the field. Ten members of Co. F went out to the monument with a photographer for a group picture, and later a very large party of the excursionists grouped along the wall and by the monument for a photograph. The spot seemed fascinating, and all were loth to leave a place so memorable to us. Meade's headquarters house, the humble, battle-scarred edifice, now restored to nearly its original appearance and condition, was visited and a good view had of the slope in rear of our position and of the Taneytown road, as shown in cut 4.

There had been a fear that with so large a party it would be difficult to

ON THE WING AGAIN. 43

induce all to be prompt, ready for starting on scheduled time, but it was soon evident the party was a live one and a business one. Long before the hour for starting away dinners had been disposed of, grips and wraps gathered and in hand and most of the people were aboard the cars; so that when the whistle sounded at one o'clock the last signal not one was absent, and the long, well laden train moved out on time. With a satisfied expression all said: "We have seen Gettysburg!"—and they set their faces southward for more delights of a kindred sort; for Antietam, the true objective point of the expedition, was just ahead. No day could be fairer, no atmosphere sweeter, and the feelings of the party were in keeping. While gaily chatting and taking in the beauties of the new scenery the people presently became aware that they were "rising in the world." Places appeared to steadily drop lower in the view and valleys to grow deeper, and what had been seen as hills a little before were beneath them. Then they discovered that they were steadily being lifted up the mountain. In winding ways they went up and up, while the views increased in extent, diversity, beauty and grandeur. At times, as at Horse Shoe Bend, were afforded loveliest vistas across wide, luxuriant valleys, and

20. Group 14th C. V. Excursionists at Monument, Gettysburg, September 16, 1891.

at times distant glimpses of miles of "Wonderland" dotted with farm dwellings and barns or clustered villages. The summit reached, Pen-Mar station was announced, and the party, leaving the train, roamed over the delectable grounds, enjoying the rare scenery their height and position afforded.

This place is situated on the line of separation of the states Pennsylvania and Maryland, the indicating board "Pen-Mar," having the "Pen" over the Pennsylvania side and the "Mar" over the Maryland side. It is the favorite resort of excursionists during the warm season from all points within fifty or eighty miles. High Rock, Blue Mountain House, and Tip Top Tower are objects of special attraction. Tourists receive this description of the locality—"A Wonderland of Nature's grandest Charms." If any people can appreciate such a winsome spot it is a set of wide-awake New Englanders, and our party fully enjoyed it, wandering in the groves of stately trees and gazing off miles away where stretched northward the valley of the Potomac, or westward the valley of the Shenadoah, or eastward the valley of the Cumberland, all an extensive prospect of charming landscapes seldom seen from one point. Not a little did the people enjoy devouring the delicious peaches fresh from orchards near and purchased for what seemed to them a song compared with prices at home. When the whistle sounded the end of the forty minutes time allowance all were promptly in their places on the train and presently sliding down the mountain towards Hagerstown. This old Maryland town, of considerable note in the war time, they rushed through in hurried style; and then the talk was, "Antietam next!" and the vet's pulses began to throb. At 4.15 the train pulled in at Antietam station, the " desired haven." This was located one mile from the village Sharpsburg. "And how are we all to get there?" was the solicitous inquiry. Well, there is a good, broad military road, one of Uncle Sam's best, running clear up to the town; and look! foresight and painstaking have done their work, and here are in waiting, like a cloud, vehicles of every description, from the simple carriage for two or three to the omnibus for twenty and those ark-like, or "prairie schooner" style, of farm wagons, with their ponderous old Maryland farm horses, ready to haul any mass of humanity. Within a few minutes all of our great crowd, for we had received reinforcements from other regiments, were, amid lots of fun at the oddity of the thing, stowed away in these vehicles and on the way to town. So thoroughly had the matter of billeting the party been attended to, that when a few minutes after the great cavalcade had driven into the village the parties in charge drove in scarcely any persons were to be seen upon the streets; they had fallen directly into their places and both people and carriages had disappeared, the latter to their stables and the former to "fix up" for supper, about ready at all the houses.

The problem had been, how could this little village, with no facilities for public accommodation beyond two or three insignificant hotels, take care of our hundreds, especially as other hundreds of other regiments were to be provided for at the same time. Parties staying but a night or two could "bunk"

THE ROULETTE PLACE.   45

in any way, but our party, composed so largely of gentle ladies, were to be away from home ten days or more of jaunting and needed good care and good resting places. The problem was solved by a Yankee device of going months in advance to the place and spending days in canvassing for accommodations among the best families of the town, and promising the people, who had several times been grievously disappointed and imposed upon and had suffered loss because of false representations as to parties, that good persons should be sent them as guests and sure pay. This, with correspondence kept up until the last day, secured us all we wanted and the best to be found. All the places could not be equally good, and

21.   The Roulette Place, from the East—Barn, House and Spring-House.

we must arrange for people as couples and as friend-groups as fully as possible, and gentlemen could put up with limitations we would not subject ladies to if avoidable; but what would the few who had cramped quarters for a hot season have said if indiscriminately the party had been obliged to bunk upon church benches and feed at improvised public tables as were many other excursionists?

It seemed befitting that our headquarters should be located " in the field " during the campaign, so quarters had been secured for our Chairman and Secretary and their wives at the Roulette house; a spot having great attraction to us not only because of its relation to our first battle experience but as

A MEMORABLE CAMP-FIRE.

Edenic in its kind, and now presided over most graciously by Mr. B. F. Roulette and his wife, worthy successors of the father and mother of the former who dwelt there during the war. Here at early evening the colors were set out by the Secretary and the Fourteenth was ready for action. By arrangement there was to be a camp-fire, not a misnamed gathering in enclosed artificial auditorium but a genuine soldiers' camp-fire in the open air, on the battlefield itself, with piles of rails—the soldier's old-time darling friend—and logs for fuel. So, when the darkness was coming on the pile of rails was kindled on the ridge close to the Roulette lane and near "Bloody Lane." Hardly soon enough was this, we confess; to anticipate the eagerness of the people, who had been supposed to be tired and likely to be late, already collected in numbers, our party supplemented by hosts of people from the town and vicinity. Soon after our huge pile began to glow grandly under its increasing flame the people gathered about on the hill-side and the effect upon them was startling. To the old vets it was a vivid and pathetic reminder of the camp-fires of long ago amid the dreary surroundings of war life and shared with the dear old comrades of those days, so many of whom had dropped out on bloody fields or perished in hospitals or starved and rotted in horrid prison pens.

22. *Blatchley.*
Roulette Lane, near Camp-Fire, looking north, toward barn.

To the ladies and civilian visitors the scene was weird, novel and exciting—entrancing. It was their first sight of what seemed a reproduction from real soldier life. At proper time our president set the ball rolling by calling for a song; and then after a pleasant speech setting forth the object of the trip, the impressiveness of the place and the memories connected with it, he called for camp-fire talks from others present. Each speaker stepped out into the full light of the blazing pile, notwithstanding risk of roasting, the scene having a striking effect upon the unaccustomed observers. Comrade Lieut. Seward gave a talk thoroughly patriotic and tender, as Miss McCarthy of the party wrote, "silent eloquence gaining the mastery as he stood in the light of the fire, one coat sleeve hanging loosely down, while with his single arm extended towards his comrades he nobly asserted that willingly would he lose that one also rather than forego the pleasure of helping to make 'one and inseparable' our glorious Union." Col. Moore, the man of fighting and deeds rather than public utterances, responded in his customary way of utterly quiet eloquence. Secretary Knowlton gave a few characteristic words of kindly appreciation of efforts of comrades. The Chaplain gave reminiscences of the regiment's movements and experiences twenty-nine years ago that day and night, and of the dreadful battle-day and the two or three days following, on this ground or near. Comrade Lieut. Lyman spoke sensible words as to our nation's momentous interests and the effects of the war. Comrade Fletcher, coming from far Kansas for the purpose of participating in the excursion privileges, gave rousing and grand words of purest loyalty and comradeship, with many entertaining illustrations. Congressman Russell made pleasant talk in humorous strain, and then most appreciative expressions of the work and sacrifices of the soldiers for the Union. Comrade Capt. Davis began one of his always delightful and eloquent talks but succumbed to indisposition and ceased; and State Senator Coffin, one of the truest of the loyal, a strong and constant friend of the soldier in war time and since, responded to his call in a hearty, feeling eulogy of the men who saved the country and of their deeds.

24.
"Bloody Lane" after the war, looking N. W.—Turn of Roulette Lane in middle ground—Dunker Church Woods in background—14th C. V. Cornfield at right of house.

It was hard to stop and thus break the spell of the rare and witching scene, but tired nature and a prospective morrow full of ardent doing of the battle-field demanded that the people should seek repose. So, with "Tenting to-night" still lingering in the air where our fervent lips had given it, reluctantly we left the spot. Of the whole affair Miss McCarthy wrote: "And as the flames shot towards heaven and you heard 'Tenting to-night' slowly, solemnly sung by those same voices that twenty-nine years ago had every reason to weep over 'Wishing for the War to cease' emotion thrilled your whole body. There was the moon (I doubt if ever, night was more beautiful), the calm, beautiful fields, overcapped by the surrounding hills; the woods through which the troops emerged on their march, and those voices swelling

48   A BIT OF HISTORY.

25. Bivouac of 14th C. V. by Boonesboro Pike September 15-17, 1862. McClellan's Headquarters on hill at right.

in one grand chorus, until the grandeur of the scene was indescribable. Another such camp-fire; another such moonlight will doubtless never be seen by the same parties."

As our people, all in their novel surroundings, sleep the sleep of the just and weary let us talk a little of the

REGIMENT AND THE BATTLE OF ANTIETAM.

The Fourteenth left Hartford for New York August 25, 1862, one thousand and fifteen strong, under command of Colonel Dwight Morris. Six companies were borne by the steamer "City of Hartford" and four companies by a propeller. The next day the men were transported by the steamer "Kill-Von-Kull" to Elizabethport, N. J., whence they were borne by a train of thirty cars, in two sections, to Harrisburg and thence to Baltimore. By another train they were taken to Washington, reaching there on the morning of the 28th. In a few hours they crossed the Potomac on the famous Long Bridge and trod for the first time the "sacred soil." This they tasted as well as trod, for it was dreadfully dusty. That night they rested on the heights of Arlington, fondly expecting a long stay in the

Elysian Fields of a "camp of instruction." Vain delusion! Before light on the 29th the long roll suddenly called them up, they received their arms, made their coffee, and shortly were tramping toward Fort Ethan Allen, Va., then threatened, near the "Chain Bridge," a few miles above Washington. Sunday, September 7th, the march was taken up with the Army of the Potomac in pursuit of Lee. The regiment was assigned with two other new regiments, the 108th N. Y. and 130th Penn. Volunteers, to form the Second Brigade of the Third Division, Second Army Corps. Daily marching brought us to Frederick, Md. by the 13th, and on Sunday "over the hills of Maryland" the march was pursued, the regiment bivouacking that night on the battlefield of South Mountain, where the dead, the first seen by us of those slain in war, were lying about. On the 15th we crossed the mountain by Turner's Gap, proceeded to Boonesboro, turned sharply to the left towards Sharpsburg, close in the wake of the enemy, and, passing through the village of Keedysville just at dark and proceeding about one mile beyond, turned into a field at the left of the road, not far from McClellan's headquarters at the Pry house, there bivouacking on the front line of the army. The next day was spent on that ground, where at one time the regiment was treated to its first shelling from hostile guns—treatment very unwelcome, as every third gun discharged sent a Whitworth bolt over the hill in our front striking somewhere in our vicinity, generally wounding some one. We saw one of these bolts take off the foot of a man across the road from us—and the most pertinent reflection about the scene was, the man struck was *out of his place*.

Glad we all were when French's battery, that had been sent flying up the road running diagonally past our front, silenced those "dogs of war." All that day it could be seen that things were being "fixed up" for a fight—leaders "cutting out work" for us—and some heavy firing just at evening by Hooker's men far up at the right settled the conviction. Soon after two o'clock on the morning of Wednesday the 17th the regiment was astir and receiving ammunition and at daylight in line. Soon afterward we crossed the road and moved, with frequent halts, around the high hill in the rear of McClellan's headquarters, about midway of the slope, making our way toward some ford of the Antietam. About 8 o'clock the ford was reached and crossed. The water was pretty deep, the banks were steep and slippery. The fording was not an agreeable recreation but we knew worse things were ahead.

We were marching that day with the Third Brigade (Max Weber's) of our division in front, our brigade, under command of our own Colonel Morris, next, and the First Brigade (Genl. Kimball's) in rear. From the ford the course was towards and then up the slope flanking the East Woods. * These woods were reached and entered about one mile from the ford and the line was at once faced to the left and advanced. Order was straightway given to form line of battle. Huge shells crashing through the tree-tops and branches and dropping and bursting about had made the men nervous,

---

* See towards right of background of cut 33.

and this order made them realize that the hour they had thought of and talked of, the hour of battle, of mortal combat, was at hand. No previous moment of life had been, to most, as serious as this. There would surely be wounding and pain and death; and upon whom of all would these come, men were reflecting. Stern duty granted no time for meditation, for the line, the deadly battle-line, was forming. General French, the division commander, seeing some halting and confusion in the brigade shouted: "For God's sake, men, close up and go forward!" The Fourteenth, Lieut. Col. Perkins commanding, was formed on the right of the brigade, the 130th

Where the Fourteenth forded the Antietam September 17, 1862.

Penn. next and the 108th N. Y. at left. Max Weber's brigade formed in our front and passed over the fence first, the 1st Del. on the right, and the 4th N. Y. and 5th Md. regiments at left of it. Kimball's brigade formed at left of our brigade and advanced later. The line well formed, the order "forward!" was given. Here the writer dismounted, sent his horse back, fell in behind Co. B and followed—and that is how he knows the things whereof he writes. His watch at that moment marked nearly 9 o'clock. Out of the woods and over the fence we went and on, one magnificent battle-line, with colors that should never again be so bright and companies that should never again be whole. Of course batteries opened on us at once, but, as usual with shelling under such circumstances, they affected the line but little. Before us was a gentle slope terminating after about one fourth mile in a swale between the houses of Mr. Mumma and Mr. William Roulette. Half way down the slope the right of the regiment passed through a corner of Mr. Mumma's orchard, and, grave as the moment was, men of Co. A plucked the fruit and ate. A little farther on that same right passed within a few rods of the blazing barn and house of Mr. Mumma, feeling the scorching heat. A little farther, and the "wee" brook coursing through the swale was reached and the line was turned a trifle to the right to advance into the cornfield, whose fence was one hundred paces beyond. Just then the left of Co. B struck the Roulette house and was detained a little to attend to some belligerent sharp-shooters sheltered there.* Then the line swept on over the fence into the cornfield, the regiment extending across its entire breadth. This field belonged to Mr. Mumma and had upon it a vigorous growth of nearly mature, tall corn with hills high heaped.

By the writer's pacing this field is about three hundred and fifty yards from rear to front. While passing through this our men were nearly hidden and but little effect of the enemy's firing was felt until we were past the middle. Max Weber's brigade reached the farther fence some yards in advance

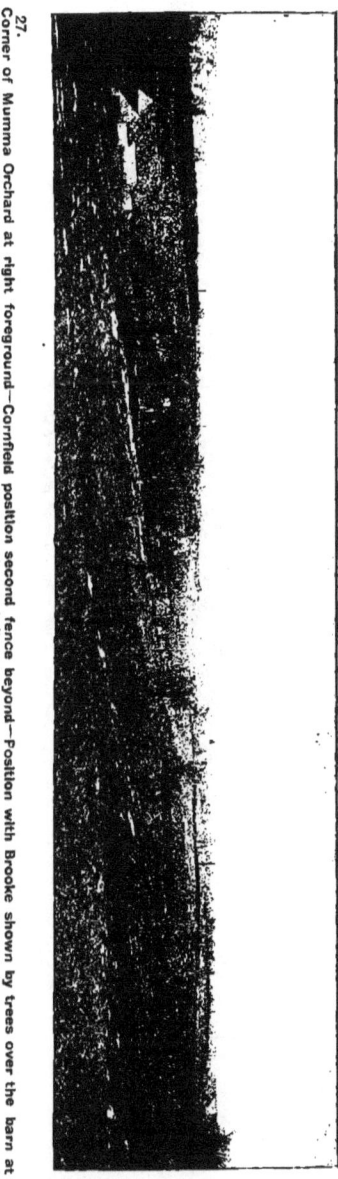

27. Corner of Mumma Orchard at right foreground—Cornfield position second fence beyond—Position with Brooke shown by trees over the barn at extreme left.

---

*Mr. Roulette had removed his family to a safe place in season, but returning himself to look after his stock he was held in limbo by the rebs. When firing began he went into the cellar for safety, but when our boys cleaned out the Johnnies he quickly ran out, shouting excitedly: "Give it to 'em!" "Drive 'em!"—"Take anything on my place, only drive 'em! drive 'em!" Then he started for the rear, for he wasn't singing just then "there's no place like home."

IN THE FIGHT.

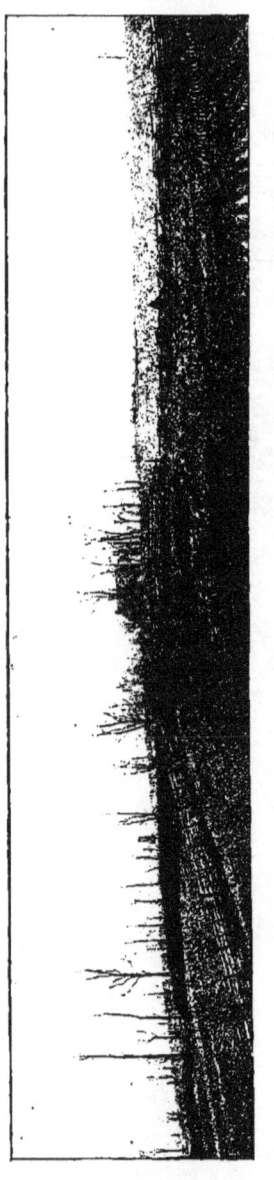

28. Fence corner, extreme left of Fourteenth in Cornfield.—Fence in front is on the Sunken Road and trees at right indicate its course.—130th Pa. was at wall, at left.—Figure is at place of Co. G.

of us and at once drew a strong fire from the enemy, which our line received a good share of from overshooting. The First Delaware men, to whom this was their first battle, stood their ground bravely, but other troops of that brigade did not do so well, as official reports confirm. Not only their wounded fell back through our lines to be cared for by us but the frightened "skeedaddlers" also in large numbers. When the Fourteenth reached the fence it received a smashing fire full in the face. This might have dashed our men's courage, but it had been screwed up to the staying pitch and they did not waver. Over the fence they went upon the clear sward field one rod, two rods, every inch of which a withering storm of bullets was smiting them. Col. Morris, Lieut. Col. Perkins* and Adjt. Ellis rode forth and back most bravely in front of the line urging the men forward; but at last, finding it impossible to advance farther, the order was given to fall back to the fence and "load and fire at will." This order they obeyed, but no farther back did they go until directed to. Stopping by the rails or dropping back a yard or two among the high corn hills, each man loaded his piece and then fired at whatever seemed a proper target. While it was very easy to *feel* the enemy it was very difficult to *see* him—and we will tell why. A lane, called the "Sunken Road," one outlet of the Mumma, Roulette, and Piper farms, leaves the Hagerstown pike about one mile above Sharpsburg, runs towards the position of the Fourteenth about one-third mile, then turns to right a little, descending a slight hill, then turns again a little and runs on

---

*Maj. Clark's nervous horse acted so foolishly that he could not urge him over the fence, and we have a vivid recollection of him among the corn hills holding the refractory beast, grinding his teeth and muttering hot expletives, until Corpl. Ed. Smith of Co. E, limping along with a serious bullet wound in the calf, led it away.

A Hidden Foe—Bloody Lane.

nearly southeast about one-fourth mile when it turns again. It pursues this crooked way until, after making six angles and seven different lines of direction, all amounting to about one right angle, it connects with the Boonesboro pike west of Sharpsburg, fully one mile and a half from the start point. This road is depressed for over one-half mile of its course, and the part from the little hill mentioned for about one-fourth mile is called "Bloody Lane." The Roulette farm lane connects with it a few rods from the foot of the little hill. This sunken part of the road men of Hill's corps had taken possession of upon retiring before our advancing division. From the left of Co. B in direct line forward to the first bend of the sunken road at top of the little hill, a little to the right of the house seen in cuts 28 and 30,* is one hundred and seventy-five paces. In this deep cut, at this near point and far up the road, the rebels were ensconced, completely concealed, in full lines, all busily plying their muskets; and on the rising ground in the field back of this position was another line so located as to fire over their heads. All these had a direct fire upon our left and a raking fire upon the rest of our line. And this was not all. Mr. Mumma's farm outlet to Sharpsburg then was a lane running along the right of our cornfield and skirting the field in our front in a circuitous course, joining the sunken road a few rods from the Hagerstown pike. From this lane directly in front of our centre to our line was about three hundred and fifty yards. This lane† had its quota of lurking infantry, and the line was extended northward behind barricades and outcropping ledges. Do our men now wonder where the heavy, deadly fire came from or why no enemy was visible, only occasionally a rusty hat?

29.

From centre to right of Fourteenth in Cornfield.

---
* This house did not exist at the time of the battle.
† This lane from the point where the right of Co. A rested to the Mumma house still exists, but all that part skirting the field in front of our position has been obliterated, the fence on our side being removed and the ground plowed. The remaining boards of the other fence have numerous bullet holes. *Who made them?*

30.
Left of 14th C. V. in Cornfield—Trees as at time of Battle.

Nothing daunted the Fourteenth men settled down to work as though expecting to stay, firing in the direction of the puffs of smoke or at anything indicating the presence of a reb. And some of them really seemed to enjoy it. We recall one sergeant as repeatedly gravely engaged in loading his gun, and then, rising and taking aim, firing; and each time there would come upon his face such a rapt expression of utter satisfaction as seemed almost seraphic. Of course many were entirely unused to handling firearms, and there were more "shots at a venture" that day in the regiment than it ever knew again, but each man did his best and bravest.

But good men were falling all the time under the incessant fusillade of the invisible foe. As they were wounded they, if unable to walk, were borne back to the Roulette house; if able to walk they could go farther back to our division hospital on the Smith farm, near our fording place. For about two hours this was continued. Sharp sense of danger was, after a time, dulled, and there was a bit of fascination in hearing the buzzing bullets passing by, or in seeing them clip a cornstalk or its leaves or strike up little puffs of dust at our feet as a running mouse would. Some of the time batteries were exchanging compliments over our heads, and occasionally one of these "compliments" would drop in our field, hoisting the earth, or, bursting in the air, would drop gentle showers of scrap-iron upon us. At one time the conduct of the Fifth Maryland affected us hurtfully. Col. Perkins says in his report that their breaking "threw three companies of my right wing into confusion. * * * during this time my right and centre were broken twice but rallied on the colors and formed in good order." From the right of the regiment, where the ground was considerably elevated, our men could see the hill * eastward overlooking the eastern section of "Bloody Lane," and they there witnessed the splendid fighting of some of the old regiments of Kimball's brigade, the 14th Indiana particularly, and later those of the "Irish Brigade" coming up in support. As they saw at one time the old veteran color-bearer crawling along the ground, his comrades moving after him in like fashion, thrusting forward his flag-staff and fixing it in the earth and then pulling

---

* Where our excursion camp-fire was.

himself up to it, the bullets flying thickly around, or at another time the full color-guard rallying around the banner as they, leading their line, charged upon the enemy, the whole line contending and gaining inch by inch until they beat the foe in their front, our men learned what veritable fighting was—and they never forgot the lesson. The spectacle was thrilling and inspiring, as Col. Perkins often remarked, and never until then had our beautiful national banner, "Old Glory," assumed its proper place in our understandings and hearts. Its bright folds, enwreathed for moments in battle smoke and at other moments reflecting the sun's glowing rays from its spotless red, white and blue floating over brave Union men risking life for it, advancing steadily against the banner of treason and disunion made a picture ineffaceable from our memories and fixed the precious emblem in our souls forever.

Some of our men at the right, as Sergts. B. Hirst of Co. D and W. H. Hawley and W. B. Hincks of Co. A, went forward from our line a little into the field with some of the First Delaware men, nearly to the large tree seen at right in cut 29, where they had a better view of the enemy's position and a better place for effective firing. When Sergt. H. saw indications that the enemy was preparing to charge he returned to his company. About this time, as the writer was approaching Co. B Capt. Gibbons inquired where the colors were. Upon being told that they were in their proper place in the line a moment before, he replied that he could not see them. A hasty run back to the centre developed the fact that the colors had been suppressed that they might not attract the attention of the enemy so much. Never again would the Fourteenth practice that kind of Yankee prudence as

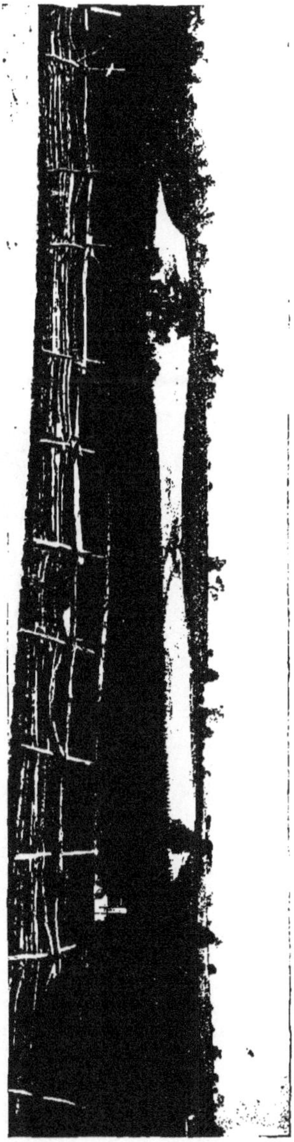

31. At left of No. 33 looking west.—Kimball's hill in foreground.—Long white field is 14th C. V. Cornfield showing transverse depression where regt. rallied.—Roulette Lane just beyond Kimball's hill.—Mumma house at extreme right.—Hagerstown Pike in background. *O. C. Gould.*

applied to matters of civil life, well knowing that for war it would not do, for men must see their colors to be assured that their line is intact and position not changed.

Just how or when the regiment was ordered to retire from this position cannot, perhaps, be known, for the companies seem not to have retired together; but the writer knows this, that when the hour of noon was near he saw Col. Morris with the colors and a portion of the regiment in a slight hollow which ran transversely of the field and the colonel asked him if he could inform him where Cos. B and G were. He replied that a moment before he had seen them at their places at the fence. "Please return to them and request them to rally on the colors here," said the colonel. The order was delivered, and soon all the companies were together and retiring to the rear of the Roulette house and into the yard between the house and barn.

32.
Roulette House after battle September 1862—West side, from swale.

Here were already fragments of other regiments and Genl. French and his staff. When the enemy perceived that our men had withdrawn they at once determined to charge over the field vacated, and they charged clear down through the cornfield and into the swale. Our two men of Co. A, referred to above, who had ultimately betaken themselves to the Mumma lane for better use of their rifles. were so absorbed in their business that they did not observe the oncoming of the rebel charging line until it was but a few rods away—then there was a sprinting match rarely surpassed. Our boys could run faster than the pursuing force yet not so fast as the cyclone of bullets sent after them by that force; but the good, brave fellows got away unharmed and afterwards rejoined their company. That the rebels reached the swale the writer can attest, for he had in care several wounded men, protected within the little basement room at rear of the Roulette house, and it looked as though all must be captured. Sergt. Tibbitts of Co. H, both bleeding arms crossed upon his breast, sat upon a barrel placidly smiling; but one man was so wrought up that he cried bitterly, exclaiming: "My God, I'd rather have been killed than to be taken prisoner by the rebels!" As we stood outside, a few feet from the door, to surrender our helpless charge if it could be done before the Johnnies shot, the foremost men in butternut came within about two rods of us, when the operations of a battery brought to bear upon the cornfield and of some infantry throwing a flanking fire into the field started those Johnnies on a retrograde movement of the most lively sort. When our division made its advance and took its first position on the field there was a gap of more than one furlong between its right and the left of where Sedgwick's division went in earlier, and this gap might have been fatal to us. It was later filled by Smith's division of the Sixth Corps, the left of Brooks' brigade of that division occupying our old position in the cornfield.

Soon after the retirement of the Fourteenth to the Roulette house an order came assigning it to the support of Genl. Kimball, some of whose regiments had been obliged to retire to replenish ammunition. It was advanced to the right, beyond the barn, to a position by a wall by the Roulette lane; which "wall" Col. Morris reports he "was ordered to take and hold," adding: "This I did with the Fourteenth Connecticut alone."*

The tide of battle was moving beyond Kimball, Richardson's division coming in for a heavy pull. This division had crossed the Antietam an hour later than the Fourteenth, and by the same ford, and had at once moved down the stream, its course for a distance restrained on the left by the stream and the rough ground along it. When the bend at Neikirk's was passed it could extend to the left, and all the brigades advanced up the slope at rear and left of Kimball, the "Irish Brigade" (Meagher's) on the right. Soon the latter brigade was heavily engaged (partly in support of Kimball), then Caldwell, then Brooke. The regiments on the extreme left, Brooke's men, advanced towards the Piper house, fighting hard and successfully, and others that had advanced beyond the line of the crooked lane faced to the right and charged upon the enemy in the cornfield and orchard between Piper's and our line, driving them and flanking the "Bloody Lane"† portion of the road, completing thus the capture or destruction of all its remaining occupants. This advance movement of Brooke on the far left made it necessary that his brigade should have support, so Kimball was directed to send him aid. As he, naturally, preferred to keep his own men, now flush with am-

---

* When our brigade was separated Col. M. invariably staid with his own boys of the Fourteenth.
† The rebels fell back to this natural intrenchment (a veritable trap it proved) to oppose the advancing movement of our forces coming over the hill. They had been steadily shot down by our determined men who had gained the brow of the hill and had a plunging fire upon them, and it was a hazardous thing for any of them to leave this road-bed and try to escape when wounded or otherwise. When the flanking movement from the left took them in reverse they were caught.

33.
Foreground hill east of Roulette barn over which 14th C. V moved going to extreme left.—E. woods where 14th C. V. first formed in background towards right.—Roulette and Mumma buildings from the east.—Cut adjoins right of cut 31.

munition, he detached his temporary reinforcements, the 14th Conn. and 108th N. Y., and sent them, under command of Col. Morris, to Brooke. This made necessary a movement of about one-half mile to the extreme left of our corps, some of the way along an exposed hill. Soon after the column started and while ascending the hill (foreground in cut 33) the regiment was subjected to a most trying ordeal. A shell from the enemy cutting diago-

34. Where Richardson fell.—The 14th C. V's farthest move to left, beyond the fence.

nally across Co. D burst in the middle of that company, killing outright Henry Tiley, W. P. Ramsdell, and R. Griswold, taking an arm from Joseph Stafford and from L. Griswold and wounding two others. Though this slaughter was sudden and terrible there was no panic—the company closed up like veterans and the regiment moved on. The movement was continued beyond Richardson's regular line to a point from ten to twenty rods beyond the fence visible beyond the hay-stack seen in cut 34. Soon it retired, by order, to the field in which the hay-stack appears and halted in a hollow at a point shown in cut 35, the left of the regiment being about where the large tree appears in the foreground. Here, though not within musket range of the enemy they were within shelling range, and some were struck. One ricocheting shell passed through the ground under H. H. Fox of Co. B, who was lying, face down, at full length. It took the breath from his body for a time and put him out of the fight for some hours. W. H. Norton of Co. A was cut nearly in two by a shell. An accident here robbed us of one of our best men, a man exceptionally well qualified for a volunteer soldier on account of his physical training, his intelligence, character, and patriotism. Robert Hubbard of Co. B. He was fatally shot through the careless handling of a rifle by a member of his own company. Another similar fatal accident happened to another promising soldier, Thaddeus Lewis of Co. A. These were not the only instances of such carelessness in the regiment though the only ones resulting seriously. The men were not yet habituated to the continuous handling of loaded guns.

A battery was stationed at the top of the hill, beyond the two large trees on the ledge seen in cuts 34 and 35, whose action it was that attracted the

35. Position at left when waiting in support of Brooke.

shelling our way. While Genl. Richardson was superintending the working of this battery he was struck, receiving a mortal wound. A detail of men of the Fourteenth helped carry him off the field. After lying in this position more than an hour the regiment was moved to the top of the hill and farther up the ridge. This was by order of Genl. Hancock, who had, upon the fall of Genl. Richardson, been directed to come from his own brigade in the Sixth Corps and assume command of Richardson's division. In his official

THE PLOWED FIELD.

report Genl. Hancock says: "Finding a considerable interval at a dangerous point between Meagher's brigade and Caldwell's brigade the Fourteenth Connecticut was placed there and the detachment from the 108th N. Y. Vols. on the extreme left." So our brigade was wholly dispersed, the 130th Penn. being still with Kimball. As soon as the regiment reached the summit of the ridge the one in command attempted to make a perfect alignment, dress-parade style. This made a royal "pot-shot" for rebel artillerymen in sight and they promptly tried it. Very soon a staff officer came dashing up and ordered the body, using a carefully selected vocabulary of words, to get down out of sight as quickly as possible. This was done; but the enemy, having the range, kept up the shelling, greatly to the misery of our men. There was only this to seriously disturb their peace as there was but little infantry firing at the right of the army after two o'clock. The heavy booming of the artillery and the crash of musketry volleys in Burnside's attack far at the left, below Sharpsburg, were heard, and there was a constant expectation of being called to action at some point. They longed for the night to come that the shelling might cease, and at last it came. The spot where they lay

36. The "Plowed Field" on Roulette Farm, Antietam. Tree tops over the hill show course of Bloody Lane.

will ever be remembered as the "plowed ground." The ground, recently plowed, had a deep layer of thoroughly dry, powdery earth. The men looked bad enough after rolling and burrowing in this, but after a rain came in the night—well, they looked like, "like everything!" All the night through and the following day and night they heard the dreadful groans and cries of the wounded and dying wretches in the Bloody Lane just over the hill calling for water, or help, or to have others taken off who, dead, were lying across or upon their tortured and helpless bodies, or for death to release them from their anguish; but they were powerless to render the assistance their hearts longed to give.

THE CASUALTIES. 61

At the Roulette house saddest sights were enacting. All day men who could not be carried further to the rear for want of ambulances were brought there and laid upon the grass or within the house, spring-house or barn. Men of both armies were there, and one could relate many pathetic scenes, inefface-

37.   Roulette House 1891—West Side, from swale.

able from memory, that occurred were there space here. Many died during the day and night and the others were cared for as well as circumstances permitted. Most of the division surgeons were back at the division hospital, but those who remained at this point were busy with whatever facilities they had for operating, our own Surgeons Rockwell and Dudley being present and constantly active. All of us were kept busy nearly the night through and renewed the work with the break of day.

Our losses were heavy. Of killed and mortally wounded there were thirty-eight, of wounded eighty-eight, and reported as missing twenty-one. Some were hit who did not leave the ranks and consequently were not reported wounded. Some of the " missing " were never heard from afterwards. Of the officers Capt. Blinn of Co. F and Capt. Willard of Co. G were shot dead at the heads of their respective commands. Lieut. Crosby of Co. K received a mortal wound and Lieut. Coit of the same company received severe wounds of both thighs that disabled him for several months. Lieut. Sherman received a serious contused wound of the side and color-bearer Thomas Mills was mortally wounded. Brave Sergt. Eno of Co. F was killed outright. Our flags were rent and gashed and one staff was badly shattered, the top being shot away. The horses of Col. Perkins and Adjt. Ellis were shot under them, the adjutant's being killed.

In the early morning of the 18th ambulances were brought up to the Roulette barn by way of the lane from the Smith farm to hurry away our remaining badly wounded, in anticipation of a renewal of the engagement. The enemy's sharp-shooters were well at work and that some of them had long-range pieces was evident, for as the writer was hurrying to the barn by the terrace walk along the garden fence to press into our service more ambulances the little rifle-sent singers in the air came so close that stooping was necessary to avoid hurt. While he was relating his experience to Dr. Rockwell, who was upon the lawn in front of the house resting from his wearying labors, the doctor suddenly sprang from his chair, as a little leaden-winged bee buzzed past his ear, exclaiming: "Well, they're after me, too!"

All that day our men lay in most uncomfortable position and exposed to a scorching sun on the plowed ground. At early light the rebel sharp-shooters began firing at every visible living or moving object. Some of them occupied a conspicuous orchard on high ground on the Piper farm in our front, firing from the trees and from behind the fence palings. We had a line of skirmishers upon the crest to look out for them. Some of these, notably those of the flank companies armed with Sharp's rifles, ensconced behind perfumed barricades of defunct horses having, as Dr. Jewett used to say, a "loud smell," did effective work, tumbling many a Johnny out of the trees. There was no engagement anywhere on the line of the army that day and it became apparent to the dullest mind that Lee must be withdrawing his troops behind this lively mask of sharp-shooters. Also, the heavy and unintermitting rumbling of wheels during the night strengthened the impression of the soldiers that the enemy was retreating. O that a Grant or a Sheridan, or even such an one as our own Hancock, had been in command of our army; some one awake and not fettered by old-time notions about regular military order nor filled with awe-inspiring visions of vast hordes of the enemy never existing! Then would all the reserves and those troops but half used yet in action have been put upon the track of the enemy—to destroy or capture, beyond a doubt.

That night our Commissary Sergt. J. W. Knowlton, having braved military regulations in order to promote the comfort of his comrades, brought a wagon-load of supplies within reach. For this he was highly complimented by officials, with distinct and strong hints of honors that should follow. But the "honors," promotion, like many another "baseless fabric of a dream" in soldier life, failed to materialize, being turned aside to others before reaching our worthy comrade.

On the morning of the 19th it was a transparent fact that there was no enemy in our front. Still the Fourteenth boys were kept on the plowed field. At last this becoming intolerable, Col. Morris, at nearly 10 o'clock, instructed the writer to go to Gen. French and state to him that the regiment had been lying in that unfavorable and trying place forty-two hours and request that it might be relieved. The "Aid" finding the general about one-half mile away comfortably located told his errand. Bluffly, with both

After the Battle.

eyes blinking at the double-quick, the general said: "Says they've been on that line forty-two hours, eh?" "Yes sir." "Tell him all the more honor to the regiment then!" It is a question whether Genl. F. had the power to relieve the regiment at that time as it was still attached to Hancock's command. When the "Aid" was returning to report his reception he met Genl. Hancock, with his staff, descending the hill, and on reaching the regiment learned that he had just relieved it and ordered its return to its own division. It was then directed to bivouac in the East Woods, about one-third mile from, and in front of, the Dunker Church. Here the men rested until the following Monday morning. They visited freely the battlefield, where they had been engaged and elsewhere, and viewed the sad havoc of war—the hundreds of the slain about the fields; the heaped-up dead in Bloody Lane; the debris of the wrecked batteries; the ruins of the Mumma buildings and the shattered walls and roof of the Dunker Church. On Sunday, the 21st, we had, in the grove, with flag-draped drums for our pulpit and our own delightful band for our sweet "church-going bell" and orchestra, our first Sabbath service in the field—

38. Dunker Church and West Woods after the Battle.

a service unusually touching, coming so close upon our recent experiences. These things, with abundant hospital work and burying our dead, fully occupied our time until Monday morning the 22d, when we broke camp, marched to the Hagerstown pike at the Dunker Church, then down to Sharpsburg and through it on our way to Harpers Ferry, most of the men never to see this land again until this day.

Well, our tale has worn the night away, and now for

THE REUNION AND THE ANTIETAM FIELD.

The magic word Antietam, more magical than any other name to most of our original men, has been holding sway in the minds of the "boys" and they are astir early and up at the Roulette house, scanning eagerly every point and place of interest they can recognize. Presently carriages bring bevies of the ladies and gentlemen of the party, and at 9.30 o'clock occurs the most remarkable reunion of the survivors of the regiment ever held—a realization of our long-cherished desire. No one can describe the emotions of the men composing that band who, recalling vividly a morning just twenty-nine years agone, a perfect counterpart as to weather of this glad, bright morning, gathered in front of the Roulette mansion. Ladies and friends, apparently as interested as the survivors themselves—for had not some of them suffered when we suffered in that long-ago time?—gathered upon the house stoop and about the lawn, adding the charm of their presence.

39. Section of Bloody Lane after the Battle.

How the business of the regimental society was attended to; how comrades out of full hearts spoke; how we sang, led by the magnificent tenor of our own Lillibridge, have they not all been told in our society's printed report, the story accompanied by the mellifluous descriptive cadences of our incomparable secretary, and sent to each comrade and excursionist? But the sentiments and feelings of that hour no one can portray. Each veteran thought of that former day this meeting commemorated, when the roar and panoply, the danger and havoc of battle were the things absorbing all attention here and this ground was moistened with the blood of comrades or of themselves; and the contrast of that with this peaceful, pastoral scene, this paradisic spot with its accompaniments, filled hearts with tenderness and gratefulness. There was deep reluctance to break up that memorable, never to be repeated, meeting, when the word "adjourn" must needs be spoken.

At once there was a grouping in front, in the outer yard, for a photograph, the men facing Tipton's camera with a little more complacency than they once here looked into the muzzles of the Johnnies' guns. Then the people betook themselves to examining the interesting premises. The quaint, solid old farm-house that bore, this bower of domestic delight, the scars of battle attracted all. Bullets pierced it on the day of battle, and one huge shell tore through the west side, a little above the floor, and going through the parlor in an upward course passed through the ceiling and a wall beyond and fell harmless amid a heap of rubbish it had created, where we saw it many times

A PARADISE RESTORED. 65

that day. During the battle the rooms were stripped of their furnishings and the floors were covered with the blood and dirt and litter of a field hospital; yet when the writer was there two weeks later, on a trip to see our wounded in the hospital near and to escort to the field a party of New Britain citizens visiting our regiment, he found it cleansed, repainted and refurnished, and Mrs. Roulette, a charming woman, presiding at a beautifully and bountifully spread table, with her husband and all her bright little ones

40. Spring-House, Roulette Place. *Street.*

41. "Bloody Lane in" 1891 looking S. E. from foot of hill.—Barricade at turn to Roulette Lane.—"Plowed Field" over hill at left background.—Brooke at middle and right background.—Piper's fields at right.

safely and cozily about her. All wanted to see the famous spring-house, with its heavy walls that sheltered some of our badly wounded, where Lieut. Crosby and others were operated on and where some of our prisoners were kept for a time—also the rare spring. in its cavity, near. The great barn that once had on its floors hundreds of hapless bodies, broken and torn by missiles aimed at the life of the nation, was explored with eager curiosity. Then the various positions of the regiment were looked over, and the fields over which it had moved from the East Woods to the cornfield and to the extreme left, with Bloody Lane, were traversed. Later in the day parties made trips to the old Dunker Church, plain but striking, that figures so prominently in all histories of the battle, and to the East Woods; also to all the

42. Dunker Church on Hagerstown Pike, Antietam, 1891.—Remains of West Woods.

significant positions on the right, guides and friends explaining the features of the field and the movements of the battle. Strange it seemed that a spirit of cupidity should have prevailed over sentiment and led to the cutting down of the West Woods (at the Dunker Church) and much of the East Woods. Later still the left of the field was visited. the Burnside bridge coming in for the largest share of attention. Upon sight of this sturdy structure, built as though to last forever, the wonder was expressed, as it had been a thousand times before, why the policy of "how not to do it" should have so long prevailed in our army; why hours should have been spent in a vain attempt to thrust a column of men across this bridge, with track not wide enough for a "column of fours" to move properly, to be subjected to a plunging fire from a large force safely covered in tiers of rifle-pits lining the cliff beyond and of the batteries commanding the road, when another and better way could have been found. It seemed a folly and a reckless inconsiderateness of human life inscrutable. Yet, as we knew the

WHERE HEROES FELL—WHERE HEROES REST. 67

story, it told for the unexampled bravery of our good Union boys warring in a matchless cause, that they would, when ordered, unflinchingly attempt such hopeless tasks. This place and its story were all the more interesting to our people because the 8th, 11th, and 16th regiments of our state were connected with the desperate undertaking here. The National Cemetery, a most sightly and charming spot, having at its centre the massive granite soldier statue cut by Batterson of Hartford and exhibited at the Centennial of our nation's independence, was much visited. Here lie in peace, mid beautiful surroundings, some of our own men who "jeoparded their lives unto the death in the high places of the field,"—this field—that our country might have the prosperity enjoyed to-day. Well wearied, and filled with thoughts of all the great things they

43.
Burnside's Bridge, Antietam, in 1862

44.
Where our boys lie at Antietam National Cemetery.

had seen and learned, many of the people spent the evening at their boarding places resting for the morrow's jaunt. A large number gave the evening to sociability and ice-cream at a public festival. The refreshments were particularly grateful just at this time, and glad we were that the church ladies wanted the money enough to prepare this festival for the visitors to their town. The 108th N. Y. and 130th Penn. regiments of our old brigade had an indoors "camp-fire" at the Lutheran church and some of our comrades attended it.

There was not much that was attractive to excursionists in the town itself, the chief interest being in the fact that it was a part of the battlefield and that Lee's army held the village during all the time of the battle. The people of the place told many stories of the disagreeable things they were subjected to, so many of them being staunchly loyal. There is a wonderful spring that pours out an unremitting stream, some inches in diameter, of pure, cold, sweet water right in the heart of the village. It is of great value to the town. From it is formed a pond by the highway, where New. Davis says he " for the first time in his life saw cows wade into the water to coax the ducks to come and pick the flies off them." The people of Sharpsburg were pleased with our party and generally

45.   *Hammond.*
The Burnside Bridge in 1891.

treated us handsomely. One lady subsequently wrote the one in charge of the billeting thanking him for sending her "such nice, good, honorable people." One avaricious old curmudgeon attempted to impose upon his guests by charging extortionate rates. He will have no more patronage or favor from the Fourteenth.

And now for

HARPERS FERRY AND WASHINGTON.

On the morning of the 18th, promptly at 8 o'clock, our people took up their journey anew and soon were on board their train bound southward, going at first over the ground trodden by Lee's army in its retreat. All were so vivacious, so devoid of indications of weariness, that one would have supposed

46. Harpers Ferry, W. Va.—Viewed from Maryland side.—Bolivar Heights in background at left.

them just starting on their trip. A run of four miles brought us to the Potomac and crossing this we were in Shepherdstown, Va. This place, often mentioned in war time, had to our New England eyes a most dismal look of unthrift and lack of care. Blackford's ford, where Lee crossed his army, is about one mile below this town.

A run of a few miles more, through a country not specially attractive, and we reached Shenandoah Junction, where the Baltimore and Ohio track was touched, and thence to Washington we were on the rails of that road Expectation was on tip-toe to see the singular town Harpers Ferry we were approaching and the oft-mentioned wild region in its vicinity. Somewhat after 11 o'clock the train rushed into the place, the excursionists observing with admiration, as they alighted, the towering bold promontory of the Maryland Heights across the

47. Street Scene, Harpers Ferry.

Potomac at their left, the higher outjutting spur of the Loudoun Heights just over the Shenandoah, and the town in front, with its scanty allowance of space for streets at foot of the steep, rugged hill on which most of it is built in the angle at the confluence of the two rivers mentioned. Although the town has improved much in recent years, especially in its upper portion, it was for a long time as during the war period, most unattractive as to its buildings and its streets. Houses of the simplest style and incommodious, constructed largely of bits of shale taken from the hill itself, nestled under the overhanging cliffs or against the ledges at the roadside. Along the river at either side of the huge hill is a contracted street. That on the right leads along the Potomac where once were the national gun factories and arsenal, destroyed soon after the outbreak of the rebellion. That on the left leads along the noisy Shenandoah, passing under high cliffs. It is exceedingly picturesque and wild, the effect heightened much by the swiftly flowing current and the Loudoun range looming up beyond it high and grand, its sides richly green with its heavy, dark foliage.

48. Where the Fourteenth crossed the Shenandoah, under Loudoun Heights, Oct. 30, 1862.

The principal street of the town runs straight up, with a narrow, rough path, nearly one mile to the top of the hill. Thence, after dipping into a slight ravine, it continues through the village of Bolivar, on a plateau, nearly another mile until the crowning ridge Bolivar Heights is reached. On this ridge, about one-fourth mile from where the road passes over it onward to Charlestown, the Fourteenth was encamped from September 22 to October 30, 1862, performing in the vicinity picket and fatigue duties. The comfort of the stay was a minus quantity, and sickness prevailed grievously; but the scenery was always attractive, rarely excelled in beauty and grandeur. Southward spread wide and fertile valley lands, parts of the Potomac and

Shenandoah valleys, dotted with thrifty farms, that at some hours of some autumn days fairly seemed like paradise realms. Northward, over two miles away, stood out, with stately effect, the Maryland Heights ridge, and but a little distance, it seemed, from its jutting front was the bold projection of the Loudoun termination; while between these two flowed with foaming tide over its boulder-filled bed the silvery Potomac, just below where it received the waters of the Shenandoah. Arrangements had been made with the proprietor of the Hotel Connor for dinners for over two hundred of our party.

The tables were ready soon after the train reached the place and they were kept filled thence on until nearly time for our departure. Many, anxious to take in all the attractions of the place possible, started early on tours of investigation on foot or in carriages. Several went up to the old camp ground on the Heights, and felt amply rewarded -- the vets. in the reminiscent gratification and others by the glorious views there furnished. Some strayed among the cozy, eerie nooks along the Shenandoah road, or visited Jefferson's Rock, a natural wonder.

49. The "Jefferson's Rock," Harpers Ferry, W. Va.— Shenandoah at left.

All went to see John Brown's Fort, the little enginehouse of world-wide fame these many years. This little building, that furnished the central setting of one of the most stirring pages of our nation's history, has, since our excursion, been removed, improperly as we believe, to Chicago as an "Exhibition" curiosity, never again to be seen on the spot and amid the surroundings most befitting it. One pleasant episode of the day was the meeting of our comrade A. F. Hall with the family of the woman who took him in and fed and washed and clothed and nursed him, so saving his life as he believes, when in woeful plight from sickness, emaciation and down-heartedness in the fall of 1862. Our grateful comrade could not forget his benefactress, and in recent years he was put into communication with her—whence came the renewal of friendship of a most pleasant character; and whence came, also, on this excursion day a banquet of choice viands to our comrade and his friends at the home of this noble, super-loyal, Good Samaritan Virginia woman and her family.

Promptly at the hour of two, the time scheduled for departure, all our people were on hand at the station. There was some delay about bringing up our "team," but none were excessively anxious to leave the romantic spot; and, the sight of the "Fort" suggesting, presently "Glory, glory, hallelujah!" was rolling out from the lips of a chorus three hundred strong, capturing the attention of all the natives and awaking the echoes of the surrounding heights. Other songs followed, for the people were aroused and happy, and when the train came backing up all clambered aboard. Then the cry was

WASHINGTON AND FREDERICKSBURG!

"John Brown's Fort," Harpers Ferry, soon after the war.

A rapid run, part of it along the Potomac and some of it in sight of the prominent Sugar Loaf mountain, so well remembered by Fourteenth men in connection with Maryland campaigns, and in two hours a sight of the noble dome of the national capitol greeted watching eyes.

About two hundred of the party were to go at once to Fredericksburg, Va. By arrangement, resident Connecticut comrades and friends met the party at the station to guide those to remain in the city to places of entertainment and those going to Fredericksburg to the Pennsylvania R.R. station, one-half mile distant. The leader had jumped into a cab and preceded these latter to announce their coming, and by the time the head of the cavalcade reached the station the tickets had been stamped and were ready for selling; and in a short time all the party had been supplied and were on board a "special," ready to start on the last prearranged advance portion of our great trip. To our own men there was decided satisfaction in the thought that they could now go into the city of bloody memories and go about at their own sweet will and stay as long as they should choose. In two hours the Rappahannock was reached and crossed to Fredericksburg. The throng hastened to the Exchange Hotel, kept by two Connecticut men, Messrs. Cotton and Hills—the former a comrade of the 21st Conn. regiment. This hotel, the only one of any pretensions in the place, had accommodations for only about one hundred people, and to stretch them to the needs of nearly twice that number, including twenty-seven *couples* requiring twenty-seven separate rooms, was no simple task, particularly as our New England people do not take kindly to the southern custom of placing several persons, even strangers, in the same room. However, with some rooms taken outside at minor hotels and private residences, and the general spirit of good nature and accommodation to circumstances prevailing, the problem was solved to the convenience of most.

The large dining room of the " Exchange" was a cheerful sight that evening with its well supplied tables and the hungry contingents of our party. Some whose eagerness could not be held in check went out for night glimpses of well-remembered places of the war time. Then old Morpheus was given sway, for jaunts of the next day were to be long ones—so while his custody of our people continues let us chat of the matter that makes this place of vital interest to us,

THE FOURTEENTH AND THE BATTLE OF FREDERICKSBURG.

The Fourteenth left Harpers Ferry October 30, 1862, and coming down the Loudoun valley to Warrenton and thence to Warrenton Junction, reached the vicinity of Falmouth, Va., November 17. At this time nearly all of the Second Corps was up, and had an attempt been made at that time to cross the Rappahannock and take possession of the Fredericksburg heights it could have been easily accomplished, as the enemy's force there was very slight. For the failure to do this there has been explanation that pontoons must be waited for and arrangements made for " change of base," but we are strongly impressed that a western army would have soon invented a plan to bridge the river and that fearless soldiery would have had no apprehensions as to keeping up communication with the source of supplies. As it was, weeks were expended in this vain waiting, giving the enemy all desirable hints as to the intentions of our leaders and all necessary time to occupy and fortify every point of consequence and to arrange troops to greatest advantage. November 18, our brigade, with the 132nd Penn. regiment added, all under command of Col. Morris, was sent to Belle Plain on the Potomac, reaching there on the 19th. Pending the completion of the railroad from Aquia Creek to Fredericksburg barges brought supplies to this place, whence they were " wagoned " to the army. Here the Fourteenth remained, in disagreeable and most unhealthful camp, about two and one-half weeks, doing duty as longshoremen in unloading barges of food for man and beast, and on picket and guarding "secesh" property; falling heirs to pneumonia, typhoid fever and other serious and deadly ailments day by day, without chance to drill or to do much true soldier work. December 6 the regiment rejoined the corps, reaching Falmouth, after one of the most wretched of marches through slush and mud, to spend a night of misery in the snow under the low drooping pines whose wood would not burn nor the branches permit the pungent smoke from the smudge to rise above the eyes of the men as they squatted or lay upon the ground.

At 11.30 on the night of Dec. 10 came an order to be ready to move on the following morning—then we knew the long expected battle was at hand. As early as 5 A. M. of the 11th the firing of heavy guns in the direction of Fredericksburg, nearly three miles below us, was heard and by 5.30 the discharges of artillery and the roll of musketry volleys were almost continuous. At six o'clock, while, amid this ominous music, Col. Perkins and his staff were breakfasting by candle light, with arms buckled on for the march and the fray, the order came to move. For the last time in camp our doughty commander's clarion tone was heard: "Fall in, Fourteenth!" and in five minutes, in the semi-darkness of the mid December morning, the regiment started. Down past Couch's headquarters, backside of Falmouth village and along the rear of the Rappahannock bluffs the line moved, the artillery's booming and the rifle's talk sounding in our ears, to a position nearly one-half mile in rear of the Lacy house, then Sumner's headquarters. It was expected that the Second Corps would cross the river early in the day and perhaps soon storm the heights. But, in this, as in many another matter in war, the "scheme" did "gang aglee;" unnecessarily, we judge, considering the great resources of our army. The old McClellan tactics had not yet run their course; nor did they until Gettysburg saw a new light.

The plan was to throw pontoon bridges across the river at three points: one about two miles below the city for the Left Grand Division, under Franklin; a second near the railroad bridge (then destroyed) for the Centre Grand Division, under Hooker, and a third a little above the Lacy house

51.
Lacy House, opposite Fredericksburg, in War time.

LAYING THE PONTOONS.

for the Right Grand Division, under Sumner. The materials for these bridges were at the water's edge at these points about 3 o'clock on the morning of the 11th Dec., and the work of construction soon began. There was a heavy fog upon the river and the immediate shores at this time. Before noon Franklin's bridge was completed, there being no opposition difficult to rout; but when the fog lifted a little soon after five and revealed the two other bridges completed to about midway of the stream an immediate destructive fire from the well posted sharp-shooters of Barksdale's brigade of Mississippians, assigned the duty of picketing the town, followed and drove the pontoniers from their work. Artillery was brought to bear upon the lurking places of the riflemen for a time and then the work of placing the bridges was resumed. This was very quickly checked again by the pestiferous and deadly work of the opponents, for the fog would not stay down long now. Several similar attempts were made at laying the upper bridge with no better success, the sharp-shooters being so advantageously posted in buildings along the river road and on Hawke street, and in the pits and trenches specially prepared. A little past noon all work on the pontoons was suspended and a general play of our artillery upon the sheltering places of the sharp-shooters and the lower part of the city ordered. For an hour or more the cannonading went on from one hundred guns posted on the bluffs opposite the city and far down the river, as well as above to Falmouth. The writer stood, watch in hand, for one hour or more upon the slope below the Phillips house, Burnside's headquarters, counting the discharges; and he found them varying from forty-six to sixty per minute. It seemed to us that the heavy bombardment must dislodge all the sharp-shooters and destroy the town; but it did neither the one nor the other. Compara-

52. Where pontoon was laid.—Foot of Hawke St. just beyond point at left.—Mander House at extreme left.—Right shore picketed by 14th C. V. winter 1862-3.—; almouth in background at bend of river.

tively few houses were seriously damaged; and as to the marksmen—well, upon a cessation of our firing and an attempt made to continue placing the bridge they came out of their holes like rats all ready to bite again. Finally, a lucky, Yankee-like thought came to some one and the bridge-laying-riddle was solved. Under cover of a heavy artillery demonstration about 3 P. M. a detachment of the 7th Mich. Vols. of Hall's brigade, Howard's division, under command of Col. Baxter, seized pontoon boats, hurried them by hand to the water,

53.
Where the Fourteenth crossed the Rappahannock Dec. 12, 1862.—Place of Pontoon at right, between the two prominent houses.

launched them, jumped into them, rowed swiftly over, leaped ashore, and forming under the bank dashed up to the top and drove the sharp-shooters near the road from their hiding places. As soon as the boats could return, the remainder of the regiment was taken over; then the 19th Mass. regiment, then the 20th Mass., then the 59th N.Y. followed. By this time the force was strong enough to drive Barksdale's rallying men up Hawke street to Caroline, where there was hot and bloody fighting until a late hour. As soon as the enemy had been driven from the river bank the bridge laying was resumed again and soon completed. This was about sunset—4.30 o'clock—and the rest of Howard's division was at once sent over.

How the Fourteenth Crossed.

Just at dark the Fourteenth was ordered forward. It had advanced a short distance over the plateau in rear of the Lacy house, some solid shot from the enemy passing over our heads, when it was ordered back and lay all night in bivouac near the army depot. That night was cold and dark. The fog and powder smoke so obscured the air that a camp fire could be seen but dimly a few feet away, giving rise to many disagreeable and annoying complications. Surgeon Jewett and the writer rode back that evening to the camp to see the sick and obtain supplies, and we learned that some of the enemy's shells had that day fallen near the hospital tent.

At sunrise on the 12th we were ordered up, and by 8 o'clock we had descended the ravine, deep and narrow, above the Lacy house, gone a few yards up the shore and crossed to Fredericksburg, our pace quickened while crossing by iron feelers thrust out of guns on the ridge back of the city to find the bridge.* Capt. Fiske ("Dunn Browne") who had been left sick at

54.
Block, Fredericksburg, Va., where 14th C. V. lay, at right, Dec. 12-13, 1862.

Belle Plain and had come up and crossed the river after the fight, told the writer in Fredericksburg that when he crossed the artillery had acquired the range quite accurately and had wounded some troops on the bridge. The regiment ascended the bank on Hawke street, turned to left down the river road, Sophia street, now A, went a few blocks and halted, the men being forbidden to leave the ranks and subject to roll-call every hour. Soon after noon it was moved up one block to Caroline street, subsequently Main, now B, then up Caroline a distance and halted on the north side of the way with the right resting on Hawke, now 14th street, and the left on Fauquier, now

---

*This bridge ran directly across the river, its head on the south side being at the foot of Hawke street, then extending to the water's edge. Mrs. Mander, living in the two story frame house near corner of Hawke and Sophia streets—see cuts 52 and 53—told the writer that she was at home in this house on the morning of Dec. 11, 1862, and witnessed the attempts at bridge laying.

13.* The arms were stacked on the walk and the men were kept at hand by the hourly roll-call. Every moment there was expectation of call to bloody engagement. At intervals there was shelling by the enemy. One shell that had passed through a chimney opposite struck, well spent, the roof of a building on our side of the street, and rolling off stopped among the feet of a chatting group of three of our men. Before their dazed senses could take in the situation it burst, wounding each one, but no one seriously—a marvelous escape. One of them, Bailey of Co. E, was so much affected for the time by concussion of both ankles that it required two of us to carry him to our division hospital, one half mile away. As the afternoon waned and the evening came on the men felt easier—life's lease had been extended one day. They had found certain common edibles in the houses, and making fires there they cooked what were to them rare, though homely, meals. Many dear friends thus took their last sup together. They lay down to sleep that night under roofs, and some on real beds—the first time in many months. Capt. Gibbons, valued and beloved of all, finding a family bible in the room where he, with fellow officers, spent the night at corner of Fauquier street, opened it and read to his associates. Headquarters of the regiment were in a little building down Fauquier a few steps. For Col. Perkins and the over hungry members of his staff, John Perkins here prepared, late at night, a meal of griddle-cakes, which, flavored with the contents of a pail of honey given the writer for our mess by a good lady near Belle Plain, made a hearty and toothsome repast—our last together. As the night wore on ominous silence full of foreboding seemed to have fallen upon the city. Our little "Perk," as he sometimes styled himself, would walk the floor uneasily, unlike his usually confident self, and occasionally break out with : " Gentlemen, gentlemen. I don't like this! Something serious is going to happen. Those gentlemen on the hill are fixing up something bad for us I fear!" And why should they not be doing so? Had they not the best position, naturally, for " fixing up " things? Had they not been given abundant time to make all needful preparation, and had we not been brought over the river and placed right in the position those gentlemen would have preferred to have us take? Let us see.

Back of the city, that had its greatest dimension along the river, was an uneven plain, slightly ascending, about one-half mile wide. Back of this was a ridge of good height, finely adapted by nature for artillery. Marye's Hill of this ridge rested on the south side of the road running out of the city as Hanover street. Willis' Hill, now the National Soldiers' Cemetery, continued the line to the deep ravine of Hazel Run, while across the road from Marye's Hill extended Taylor's Hill, sweeping above in a curve toward the town. These hills were well packed with the best batteries of the enemy, as closely placed as possible for effective working, and their slopes

---

* This was something of a *business* block before the war, having both stores and dwellings—now business has gone down the street. The large dwelling at corner of Fauquier st., where Capt. Gibbons had quarters, was burned after the war. Houses standing there now (shown in cut 54) are new.

were lined with deep rifle-pits. The guns had a good direct fire upon the plain and the town, sweeping every cross street, and most of them a good enfilading fire upon much of the field, while the amphitheatre-like formation of Taylor's Hill gave the guns there a cross, or flank, fire upon all points of the plain. At the foot of Marye's Hill and extending far southward was the sunken, or "Telegraph," road, about twenty-five feet wide, with a stone wall, shoulder high to a man, along its lower side, an embankment on the outer side of this wall reaching at some places to its top. One cannot conceive a stronger position for infantry in defense. In this road were posted two or more ranks of men, easily reinforced, who could keep up a continuous blaze of musketry upon any advancing opposing lines in almost absolute safety themselves, while along the terraced hillside back of them rifle-pits held ranks of men who could fire over their heads, the artillery on the brow of the hill firing over the heads of all. This was the situation at nightfall, Dec. 12, 1862.

One may as well allude here to the stories sometimes told of looting and wanton destruction of property by our troops. The writer's very good opportunity for observing in many streets during all the stay of our division in the city fails to confirm these stories; and he did not hear any such stories while *in* the city. Beyond the using of flour and other provisions for food and the proper use of household articles, always justifiable under such circumstances, with some instances of taking slight articles of little value as mementoes, he saw almost no pilfering, and no wanton destruction. Positively, the charge cannot hold against the men of our regiment. There were instances of jolly fellows of the Irish Brigade, and others, rigging themselves out in the toggery, old stuffs out of date, found in ladies' wardrobes, and, with parasols raised, with mien and airs and mincing step of fashionable belles or quaint old demoiselles, promenading the walks of the blocks where quartered, such being the limit of their range. This was simply the spirit of eternal youth exemplified; the thing that kept men's hearts from "failing them." Genl. Howard, who was in the city with his command all the night ahead of us, mentions this kind of foolishness, with a little pilfering, and says that while "many poor people had remained in the city and many had come to our people for protection no instance of personal abuse or violence came to my ears." Fredericksburg people left very little portable that was *worth stealing* when they quit the city before our army entered. They had received long warning and had well improved it.

About nine o'clock on the morning of the 13th December came the order for the Fourteenth to fall in. Moving by the right flank and filing left the regiment marched up Hawke street one block to Princess Anne, now C, street, then down the latter about five blocks to a point between the court-house and a church edifice, receiving at each cross street a fire from the batteries back of the town. The court-house steeple was used as a signal tower during all the regiment's stay here and until late that afternoon. Official reports of signal officers show that this was the only place in the city used for such a purpose that day. The signal flag was in motion nearly all the time and of course attracted frequent shots from the enemy's batteries. Shells struck buildings near, sending flying bits of brick and timber and of themselves all about, and many soldiers near us were struck and horribly mutilated in our sight. The men's hearts fluttered in unison with the movements of the signal flag vibrating over their heads, for well they knew that some of its swayings would yet spell out an order for them to advance ; and this waiting, waiting in suspense, amid such surroundings and with such apprehensions as came to them, seemed worse to endure than a dash upon the field.

55. Court House, Princess Anne St., Fredericksburg—Signal Tower during the battle.

A portion of the Left Grand Division had crossed the river early, and on this day some of the troops had advanced and attacked Jackson's men on the rebel right. They had been successful in breaking the lines and driving the enemy some distance. Then, according to subsequent confessions of some of Jackson's officers, the enemy's ranks were seriously demoralized, and had Meade been reinforced with five thousand fresh men, to be followed by ten thousand or fifteen thousand more—and there appears no good reason why he could not have had these or even a larger number—he could have followed up his advantage gained and have swung around into the rear of Longstreet's position and taken in reverse the whole line in our front, so making necessary the abandonment by Lee of all the heights in the rear of the city. But nothing of the kind was done. Meade was not reinforced, the advance at the left was stayed and our troops there were obliged to fall back; and just that thing was done that ought not then by any means to have been done—the attack on the right was ordered.

The signal flag above our brave boys' heads said that French's division must prepare to advance, as it was to lead the attack. The details had already been arranged and it took but brief time to set the columns in motion.

At the rear of the city there was, and still is, a canal or race-way, of width varying from eight to fifteen feet, conveying water from the river above the town to mills below. This was crossed at certain streets by narrow bridges, from some of which the planks had been removed by the rebels, leaving but little more than the stringers. Over these all our attacking parties must pass and numerous guns of the enemy's batteries were trained on each.

56.
Old Depot, Prussia St., Fredericksburg, Va.

At 12 M. the flag that all were so intently watching ceased its ominous flutterings. "Forward!" was the cry. Of Kimball's brigade, which was to lead, the 8th Ohio, 4th Ohio and 1st Del. regiments (the last one temporarily attached) were sent forward as skirmishers. The 8th Ohio moved out at the right on Hanover street and when outside of the city deployed to the left to connect with the 4th Ohio and 1st Del. that had moved out by Prussia street below and deployed to the right. Soon afterward the rest of Kimball's brigade moved out by Prussia street and advanced upon the plain, presently followed by the Third Brigade, Col. Andrews commanding. Then came the order for the Second Brigade,* our own, to advance. Like a

---

* Col. Palmer of the 108th N. Y. commanded the brigade that day, Col. Morris having been left sick at Belle Plain.

bugle note sounded out Col. Perkin's call: "Forward, Fourteenth!" Down Princess Anne the regiment hurried, amid the sound of arms upon the field and the crash of shells falling in the streets or bursting in the houses, receiving at each intersecting street a galling fire from the batteries on the Marye and Willis hills. Prussia street reached, facing the old brick depot so well remembered since, the command filed to right and moved out that street one block, covered on the right by the houses, until the dreaded canal was reached and the bridge touched—then the storm burst upon them. The rebel gunners had the exact range. With abundant time to calculate distances they knew just where to drop their shells and how to time their fuses. The batteries in front had opened all along the line, and as the regiment could go but slowly over the bridge the missiles did murderous work.* On the

57.
The Fatal Bridge, in foreground looking towards Princess Anne St.—Old R. R. Depot seen beyond the car at right, 1891.

bridge fell good David Lincoln of Co. B, both legs knocked off above the knees, and Daniel Otis with a fatal wound. Into a "slaughter pen," indeed, were the men going, but with brave hearts they pushed forward, the officers cheering them on. Soon they filed to right by a half wheel, for this road was far to the left of the point to be charged, until the line came under the partial shelter of a slight mound, and formed on the left of Andrews. One or two changes having been made here to conform lines to positions, instructions were given the men to lie close until ordered up. The guns on Taylor's Hill fairly enfiladed the position doing deadly work, particularly at the left

---

* Sergt. Hincks, close at the head of the line, thus graphically described: "Canister shot went hopping round the depot yard and on the causeway like enormous marbles, and shells burst, with a hideous crash, on every side."

of the regiment, as they did in the 10th N. Y. near. It was a moment when men's hearts are stricken with a dreadful expectancy, for the outlook was horrible. Kimball's veterans were ordered on, and, bracing for the fray, they made their straight, fierce rush at the stone wall; to be hurled back by the leaden storm flung out at them by tiers of musketry as barks are beaten back by raging gales. Then Andrew's brave fellows were ordered up to the charge, to meet a similar fate. There was a rush, a cheer, a crash of musketry with a tempest of bullets driven straight at their breasts, and the line dissolved, stragglers or clusters firing here and there, but chiefly dropping upon the ground to be exposed as little as possible. Then the Second Brigade was ordered "up and at 'em!" Ah, that charge! A few rods brought the line to the flat ground directly in front of the old "Fair Grounds," indicated at that time by some remaining tall posts and some high boards clinging here and there to the rails.* Here Col. Perkins shouted his last command to the Fourteenth. He dashed ahead and his brave boys followed. A few rods, over ground every foot of which was lashed by artillery, and the leveled guns on the direful wall coolly waiting spoke out in unison terrific. Down went the leader, down went Major Clark, Capt. Carpenter, and Lieut. Hawley. Capt. Gibbons and Lieuts. Stanley and Comes went down with mortal wounds and Lieut. Canfield was killed outright. Other officers were slightly wounded and Sergts. Fiske and Foot received frightful wounds; and so fell Color-bearer Dart and hosts of good men of the rank and file. On pressed the rest as though thinking to encompass victory by their daring, reaching to within one hundred and fifty yards or less of the wall, when, hopeless of success, most dropped beside the huge fence posts or into little hollows for slight protection and to use their guns as best they might against the foe. While lying by one of these posts, Sergt. Dart and Corpl. Symonds of Co. D received fearful face wounds. A shell struck the ground near them and exploded. A fragment tore off most of the face of Dart, frightfully disfiguring him for life, and the sharp sand was driven into the eyeballs of Symonds, quenching light there forever. Sergt. Lyman of the same Co. was lying close by these when they were hurt but strangely escaped harm, and with others put in some good work with the rifle. This was to our division the real end, and it practically dropped out of the fight for the day. Hancock's division, that crossed below the railroad bridge, was soon ordered up, to go through the motions; doing some splendid fighting, and apparently gaining some advantage at one time; meeting extraordinary losses and in the end succumbing like French's division. Then Howard's division took up the cue, sharing at the wind-up, toward nightfall, the same fate as the preceding divisions. There was some more attacking by other troops but it availed nothing as to conquering the position.

From Hancock's success at one or two points, putting the enemy to sore

---

*The present owner of this ground told the writer that the Fair Ground contained ten acres and that he purchased it and built his house exactly at its centre. Fourteenth men can calculate (see cut 58) how near they were to the "sunken road."

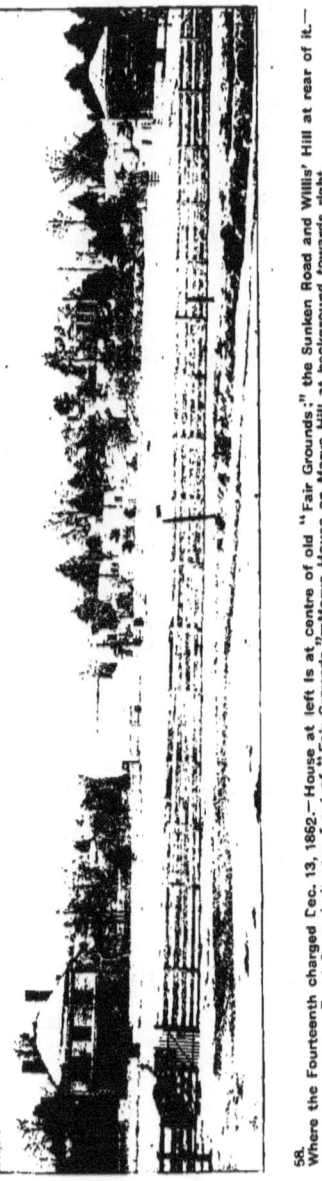

58.
Where the Fourteenth charged Dec. 13, 1862.—House at left is at centre of old "Fair Grounds;" the Sunken Road and Willis' Hill at rear of it.—Front fence indicates front of "Fair Grounds."—Marye House on Marye Hill at background towards right.

straits and causing him severe losses, we judge that had there been an attack in mass by all the divisions of our corps a breaking through the enemy's line at some point might have been effected and the heights gained, but by the dribbling, brigade order of the attacks no appreciable hurt could be caused by one charge that the enemy could not repair before another onset came.

How our men got off the field it is hard to tell. Finding it a useless and murderous exposure of themselves to stay they drifted off singly or in little squads as lulls in the storm or the clouds of smoke gave them opportunity, helping off such wounded as they could. Some, sheltered in trifling hollows, waited until night came down to conceal them and then went off. In a large excavation, the ruins of an ice-house, well towards the town, a large number stopped, until, with men of many regiments, the hole was full. From this place Sergt. Lyman backed into town at evening the badly wounded Gready of his company. In the rear of the square brick house above the right of the Fourteenth (see right of cut 58), where Kimball's men charged, men pressed for protection until the mass looked like a huge cluster of swarming bees extending far back. Presumably, none of the Fourteenth were there. For once one of our colors came near being lost to us. F. B. Doten and W. B. Hincks of Co. A inquiring of Col. Palmer as to the whereabouts of their regiment, he could not tell them but pointed to a flag lying on the ground near. This proved to be our state color. Falling thus, in a timely way, into the right hands, it was borne from the field and saved. The bodies of some of Kimball's men were found and recognized near the Ebert house, within thirty or forty yards of the wall. How near it

THE VICTIMS.   85

some of the Fourteenth men may have gone we can never know; perhaps as near as Kimball's men or nearer, for the foremost were never seen after the charge nor were they heard from again. None of those reported missing *on the field* ever came back. It is probable that not a man of the regiment was captured, and it is stated and believed that not a man of the Second Corps was. When the night fell, and on the morning after, the ground in front of the wall was strewn with forms in blue; but the morning after our troops withdrew, as said a woman living near the wall, "the ground was white." They had been stripped.

The losses of the Fourteenth in killed and mortally wounded numbered forty-four; wounded, as known, seventy-one; missing, five—fully one-third of the number taken into the fight. Remnants of the regiment rallied at the

Rowe House, Fredericksburg, Va.—Hospital Dec. 12-15, 1862.

river side, below the railroad bridge, under Capt. Davis, then the ranking officer.

The scenes and the work at the hospitals were appalling. Men had been borne to church edifices, ware-houses, and various public and private buildings until the city seemed full of the wounded, though numbers of those able to walk had gone over the river. A large proportion of the wounds had been made by shells and were of a ghastly character. To our division hospital, the Rowe house on the river road, men were brought until rooms, verandas and lawns were full. Under the large sycamore in rear of the house our surgeons plied the knife, saw, and forceps and applied ligament and bandage until far into the night. On the northern porch lay, among others, our Dart, his face torn off as though slashed away with a cleaver, and by his side lay Symonds, his eyes swollen with inflammation to the size of eggs, the sand grains showing through the tightly stretched and shining lids. Near the south porch lay our Lincoln, his two legs dangling from the trunk by naught but the slender cords. Though the sight of his poor, mangled form forced out our tears, his smile was beatific as he gave us words of love for his young wife and friends and expressed his devotion to his country and his readiness to die. We buried him in the garden, taking sixty seconds of precious time for a little service at his grave. In a room above lay, pale as death with his grievous wound, the noble Stanley, and near him Sergt. Fiske, with that rent in his stomach that, though, as he said, not "as big as a barn door nor deep as a well," kept him groaning all the night. And there was Carpenter; also Lloyd, who, though grimacing with the pain of a shattered wrist, would keep his jokish tongue wagging in a way that seemed ghastly just then; also many others. In a little building just above were, with others, Col. Perkins and Major Clark, the former suffering so from what then seemed an unexplainable wound of the shoulder that it required our steady effort until long past midnight to reduce his sense of pain sufficiently for him to sleep. In the yard, under the sycamore, were two large cauldrons set in masonry. These held a barrel or so each and had been used by Mr. Rowe for trying out fats. The division surgeon, Dr. Grant, had entrusted to the care of the writer all the tea, coffee, sugar, and spirits in the medical supply wagon, with the injunction to see that all were used with the utmost carefulness; especially the spirits, of which there were only a few bottles. It required vigilance to prevent the very dry, the thirsty *for* spirit, the grievously unwounded from snatching sups of the latter, and every drop was needed for our badly shocked sufferers. When a suggestion was made that we utilize the cauldrons for brewing the tea and coffee for the sufferers there were many willing hands to bring water and make fires and do the brewing. As we went about at a late hour with details carrying buckets of the precious drinks and the surprised men were told to take all they wished of the refreshing cup the benedictions that followed were so flavorous of genuine gratification and gratefulness that they remain with us one bright memory of that dismal night. In the morning, apprehensive of a renewal of the fighting,* we sent over the river all the wounded. Col. Perkins. Major Clark and others unable to walk being borne on stretchers. Then Drum Maj. McCarthy and the writer started on a tour of the hospitals to find Capt. Gibbons and others of the Fourteenth said to have been taken to a church and other buildings on Princess Anne street; but we found that they had already been taken over the river and were safe.

There was little firing that day except by the pickets and but few were wounded. The regiment rested by the river, the number increased now to nearly two hundred. It was not a pleasant or healthful spot to repose on.

---

* In proof of Maj. Clark's word that " no one could be safe in the city " we state, that one shell went through the roof of our building; one passed within a few feet of Lincoln as the writer was bending over him; we saw one burst in the road near in a group of batterymen and their horses; one burst in the air over our head and one tore a shoe from a foot of the writer's horse in a stable near. These are specimens.

for mother earth, their only seat or bed, was wet and soft and cold, but it was pleasanter and *healthier* than a position before the stone wall.

Early on the 15th the hospital force was ordered to return to the north side of the Rappahannock and all of our portion went except Surgeon Jewett,* who was detailed to stay with the regiment, and the writer, who stayed from choice. At evening of the same day the regiment was ordered over, and late that night it reached the old camp above Falmouth in a dreary rain, the men weary of body and depressed in spirits. Before daylight of the 16th all our forces recrossed the river, the city was abandoned and the pontoons were cut loose from the southern shore—and the enemy had not come out of their entrenchments to pursue.

But the day has come again and our people are moving about to see this

A bit of the "Sunken Road."

Fredericksburg we have been talking of. Eager to see some of the places once indelibly burned into their memories our "boys" have started to find the place of the pontoon ; the block on Caroline street where they buckled on the harness for the direful struggle, and Princess Anne, where they awaited the final summons to the encounter ; the fatal bridge over the ditch ; the storm swept plain ; the Marye house, so plainly visible from the Stafford hills while we were there and always since the war of such historic eminence ; the hospital building, red in memory, and the Lacy house, now heavily embow-

---
* Surgeon Rockwell had been left sick at Belle Plain and was not with us at all, but Asst. Surgeons Dudley and Jewett had staid in the city from the beginning.

ered in trees of a sub-war growth. While some of us were at the place of the famous wall, with an *inside* view, the writer ventured the assertion that for desperateness as related to the attacking party and for strength of position and immunity from danger of the defenders the much-lauded charge of the 3rd July, 1863, at Gettysburg did not compare with the Union charges here December 13, 1862. That at Gettysburg there was but *one* charge, comparatively brief, of one vast body of men, larger probably than our whole corps here, the vastness giving to each person of it a ground of confidence for victory and a sense of mighty companionship, so helpful in a desperate undertaking, the defending force drawn out to an attenuated line on a ridge of slightest elevation and with only a simple wall as a defence in some places and no barriers in others, all this force exposed when the contest was well on; while here the charges were made in piecemeal order of small brigades and over a plain literally raked and swept by fresh, fully-prepared artillery from its outer edge to its front, and said front mowed by musketry, the defenders, several ranks deep, almost wholly concealed behind an impervious high wall and backed by well-manned rifle-pits higher located and by closely placed artillery; and he inquired if others, upon now comparing, so judged. There was a unanimous acquiescence in the opinion. "And," added our Broatch, "we can judge of the difficulty of taking this position by just imagining the old Second Corps occupying it. How many men do you suppose could take it from us?" "Not thirty thousand!" was the reply.

In the morning paper our men found this greeting awaiting them under double-headed lines: "The Yanks again with us. Old Union veterans visit the places they helped to bathe in blood." And some old fossils snarled their bitterness as some people showed us civility and hospitality, causing astonishment to some of their friends who "thought the wah was over"—but it could not hurt our feelings at all nor depress our spirits, especially as many good citizens and some old Confeds. welcomed us warmly. One of the latter chatted an hour or two with a group of us over the war and its causes, expressing his present satisfaction at the outcome and his conviction that none of his class could be again duped into such a struggle. Then, as he told us, he knew nothing of the northern people and their intentions except from garbled misrepresentations, for no newspaper that could enlighten them could come into their hands. "Now," said he, "I take a northern paper all the time, and I read it, and my old comrades do the same, and we know you now and cannot be deceived again."

This town of ancient note and early importance, for years of late so dull, had in it but little of interest to see. There were some pleasant residences, and a little enlivenment was apparent in some newly started factories. Mary Washington's homestead in the city, and her much mutilated monument and outrageously neglected tomb, came in for a share of attention. That ourselves were objects of curiosity to some of the people was obvious. When our Kansian contingent, comrade Fletcher and his wife, were out observing, a little girl who spied the unctuous, smiling face and substantial form of our comrade clutched excitedly her mother's gown, exclaiming: "O maw, come

SURPRISES.   89

and see the Yanks!" Lieut. Fiske, "our Fiskie" as the boys affectionately call him, had a genuine treat. A poor old darkey from the country came down the street with a small load of wood on a bit of a cart drawn by a diminutive steer in harness made of bits of rope. "What will you take for your load, uncle?" called F. "Half a dollar sah," was the reply. "Half a dollar for all that? I'll take it!" Then photographer Sweet of our party was sent for and driver and outfit were "took." Then the hat was passed around and numerous "chink" dropped into it and the old man was told to take his wood and sell it again. He had the surprise of his lifetime and went away laden with funds and happiness—and Fiskie was happy. The lieutenant expressing a wish to find the building he was taken to when wounded, he was promptly conducted there. When introduced to the present owner

61.
Chancellor House, Va., and Orange Plank Road, 1891.—From the West.

and occupant, a comrade Fleming, and shown the room where he spent his wretched night after the battle he was exuberant with expressions of delight. He pointed out the spot where he lay and told a story characteristic of his modesty and self-abnegation. It was, that when he had been laid upon the hard floor some persons brought in a mattress for the use of a badly wounded officer they were about to bring there. While they were gone for this officer he, having with his longing eyes taken in the advantages of pre-empting the mattress, managed in some way to flop himself to and upon it; and when the party came bearing in the other man to place upon it they found, to their astonishment, our modest friend there—simply unconscious of their presence and suffering dreadfully! Being told that the floor had still upon it great blood stains the lieutenant exacted a promise from Mr. Fleming that if the boards should be taken up he would send him one.

Before noon large parties were made up for a trip to Chancellorsville, ten miles away. Others started out to find the old camp above Falmouth. All at Chancellorsville were greatly interested in the Chancellor house, a relic and waymark of the battle. The eastern wing of the structure was burned during the battle and when the ruin was repaired this portion was not rebuilt; also a "mansard" replaced the old steep roof.

There is an open space in the forest on the river road, about one-third mile at rear of the Chancellor house. The same ground was open at the time of the battle. The Fourteenth left the old camp at Falmouth April 28, 1863, crossed the Rappahannock at United States Ford at evening of the 30th and bivouacked that night on this open field, about two miles from the river. The next day, leaving here knapsacks under guard, it advanced with the division a mile or two beyond the Chancellor house southward on a reconnoissance in force, returning to this spot that evening—to be, as our boys will remember, the recipients of a lively shelling just after our band struck up "Hail Columbia." At evening of May 2, when the Eleventh Corps broke and our division was ordered up to check the advance of Jackson, the regiment, again leaving here all knapsacks under guard, advanced to the Orange Plank Road, and, turning to right past the Chancellor house, hurried, just at dark, about one-half mile up the road and filed into the woods at the right. It was an exciting and most critical time with our army. The regiment held this position all that night of turmoil and apprehension in front of the place where Jackson fell. In the morning, after considerable severe fighting and some serious losses, as the enemy was flanking it the regiment fell back through the woods, happening upon this identical bit of open ground again. On the night of May 4, 1864, at the opening of the Wilderness campaign, the Fourteenth once more bivouacked close to this same field. As this spot was so attractive, a squad of the members of our party went out to it, and thence retraced the steps of that morning of May 3, 1863, going through the woods to the place where the regiment was engaged, a little distance from the Jackson statue. The ground was readily identified. There yet existed traces of the battle and our party picked up bullets and other relics. An association has purchased most of this portion of the field to make a great and permanent battlefield park. Comrade Inglis and his wife, whose enthusiasm and endurance rivaled those of the hardiest vets., drove four miles further to the Wilderness battlefield. Comrade Blatchley and his son did the same—whence our views 62 and 63.

To those who had set out to find the old camp it proved, as it had proved to others before, a "fickle jade" and entirely eluded their search, greatly to their disappointment. There being a strong desire to see that old spot of so many sombre and some genial memories, the next morning a party in six carriages, under the guidance of one who had been there, started for it. Driving a mile above the city, we crossed to Falmouth village on a fine new iron bridge and thence went two or three miles up the Hartwood Church road. When the way to the camp was shown there was small surprise that its labyrinthine locality had foiled so many seekers. When, standing on the side

THE OLD CAMP AT FALMOUTH.   91

hill of the camp, the lower half of which is cultivated, the guide pointed out the brook coursing in the dell at its foot, the camp of the 12th N. J. regiment beyond and that of the 130th Penna. just around the turn, the place of brigade headquarters and that of the commissary department beyond it, and various other points, and then stepping into the growth of young trees covering the upper part of the hill and pointing to the old hut excavations and the company streets between them asked if the evidences were sufficient, all the "boys" said: "It is the old camp, sure enough!" "And yet," said Broatch,

62.   *Blatchley.*
Where 14th C. V. colors crossed the Orange Plank Road, May 6, 1864, Battle of the Wilderness.

"if we can find the places where the officers' Sibley tents stood the chain of evidence will be complete." "Very well, let's go right up." So up

63.   *Blatchley.*
Brock Road, Wilderness, Va., where 14th C. V. colors were planted May 6, 1864.

the street of companies B and G we went to the top of the hill, where a perfectly preserved circular ridge, the base of one "Sibley," appeared. A little farther up the line another such base was found, and so all five in their course—and the chain was complete. Those little mounds and hut excavations, awaiting all the long years past our coming, were mutely pathetic of a winter of hardship and gloom enough for a decade of life. Long may the kindly woods be allowed to remain to preserve them for us. The old parade ground above the hill was found to be covered with a thick growth of trees and shrubs. Beyond this a little, cozy white house was pointed out and the comrades inquired of what it was. They responded promptly: " French's headquarters." On the upper side of the hill were shown several narrow, deep excavations, touching reminders of regimental burials in the dark war days. Mr. Gibbons of the party was taken to the place where the broken body of his father, our Capt. Gibbons, and that of Lieut. Comes had received temporary burial one bleak December day in '62. It was a military funeral in full. All the regiment turned out, the chaplain officiating and the band playing a dirge. This spot had a hallowed interest to the young man and a sight of it touched him deeply.

After the visit to the camp we drove to get a view of Couch's headquarters, and then to the high hill overlooking Falmouth where the 20-ppdr. Parrott guns stood that threw their long bolts into Fredericksburg during the battle. Comrade Miles of the 27th Connecticut was highly gratified in finding the old camp of his regiment. That afternoon the same party went over to the old Washington homestead on the heights below the railroad bridge, and went to the position there of the battery of seven 30-ppdr. Rodman guns manned by two companies of the First Conn. Heavy Artillery during the winter of '62 and '63. These guns could have helped us much on the day of the battle had the gunners been allowed to serve them as they wished—so the writer was informed by them once when there soon after the fight. Sergt. Spencer and others went that day to Spottsylvania and the " Bloody Angle "—about the bloodiest place history notes—where the Fourteenth had one of its serious engagements. Here an oak tree more than a foot in diameter was actually cut down by the bullets shot across it, so close were the contending lines it was between, so numerous the shots and so fierce the fighting. That evening nearly all the remaining excursionists returned to Washington, for each desired to devote all available time to " doing " that city.

A very attractive object to all the guests at the " Exchange " was the museum of war relics collected by the proprietors of the hotel and arranged for display in the large sitting room. This was the finest collection of its kind in the country, comprising small arms and missiles, accoutrements and gear of nearly every description—muskets and sabres, bayonets and bullets, pistols and lances, shell and shot, canteens, knapsacks, belts, buttons, shoes, uniforms, ensigns and gauntlets, many of them of strangest styles and nearly all picked up on the battlefields in the vicinity. There were sections of large trees in which were imbedded solid shot or shell, and there was a section, several feet high, of one tree that had the appearance of a gigantic sponge or filter. To think of men of human flesh and bones and blood standing before the same kind of battery fire of grape and canister that had riven that tree! Some of the relics were exceedingly rare and valuable. It may interest our people to be informed that since our visit the whole collection has been sold and taken away.

It is surprising what an amount of endurance people develop. Four or five days of such excursion jaunting, walking, riding long courses, seeing, hearing, investigating and talking, and of staying in strange places with many strange "inconveniences" would seem enough usually to take the enthusiasm out of any such party, but most of our excursionists appeared to never tire. Not a moment was lost from bad weather from the start. Clear

64.   The National Capitol, Washington—East front.

skies and fine air, albeit growing hot and dusty at last, favored every hour of every day and night—and the people made the most of it. All had come to our national Mecca, our unrivaled capital city, to see all it could show them, and our vets were eager to view all the places known to them during the war, noting the astonishing improvements. While the city is not so vast as some of our metropolitan cities it is a place of marvelous beauty as to the order of its laying-out and its adornments, the width of its streets and the smoothness of their pavements, its arboreal furnishings and the fine statues of our national heroes occupying the many public squares and circles. Some of our enthusiasts took them all in. They visited the capitol, vast and grand, with its immense halls of legislation; its great rotunda, with choice historical and allegorical paintings; its immense congressional library; its "seat of judgment," where the highest court magnates of the land hold sittings; its basement, with most exquisite frescoes, and its lofty, symmetrical dome, from whose top they could see the city at their feet, its avenues radiating from them like the spokes of a wheel. They called at the White House, executive mansion and presidential residence in one, and passed through its elegant apartments, seeing some of the dignitaries of the land—simply human beings. They went to the massive pile of granite called the Treasury, and had a peep, if they chose, at the heaps of "tin" in the vaults, and to the elegant granite structure where the business of the State, War, and

65.
Executive Mansion, "White House," Washington.

Navy Departments is attended to, a building said to be the finest structure in the world devoted to such purposes. They ascended the needle-like Washington Monument and from a dizzy height had the view of views. The famed Smithsonian exhibited to them its treasures archæological, ornithological, and entomological, while the Museum of Natural History afforded them hours of delight and instruction with its immense and rare collection of curious and illustrative articles. Here were relics of the persons and homes of our illustrious Washington, Grant, and others. Here were collected specimens of the precious materials for useful structures and implements and for ornamental purposes, and of the mineral, vegetable and animal products of our great country and of the seas. Here were specimens of the industries of the nations, from the culinary utensils, the boats, the musical instruments, the carvings, the fabrics of the most rude peoples to the finest products of hand or machinery of our own first-class nation. Not least interesting in this great repository was the famous Catlin collection of painted Indian portraits and scenes from Indian life—a collection wonderful in its kind and that could not be replaced if lost. The Corcoran Art Gallery, with its choice collection of paintings, copies of antique sculptures, ancient gems, carvings and rare bronzes captivated the artistic. Most made the American patriot's pilgrimage to Mount Vernon to see the home and haunts and tomb of our immortal Washington. This place, as delightful as it is noted, always charms the visitor. Yet there is something more than the view of beautiful scenery and rare old curios that affects the true American heart here—it is the gratification of a lifetime longing, a reverential desire, to see the place where lived, thought, spoke and trod the man our early chillhood held in veneration.

Great Arlington, too, with its sacred acres bearing on their bosom the precious dust of sixteen thousand of our heroes who perished that the nation might not be disrupted, was a place of absorbing interest. Not only did the multitudes marshalled, as the little headstones indicated, in the eternal "bivouac of the dead," hold their attention and their hearts' homage, but the grounds of varying plain and dell and grand old forest trees and charming floral growth, and the broad and perfect roads, direct and winding, all delighted them.

66.

Mount Vernon, Va.—Washington's Home.

Little by little the number of our party diminished, some forced home early by pressing calls of business or duty, others lingering as long as possible, until by the 24th nearly all had left the city and gone home ; there to recall and repeat with unabating pleasure the incidents of their delightful trip—a trip which our Hall calls, in his "Souvenir Album," "Our delightful and long to be remembered excursion; so ably planned and so successfully executed."

A battlefield historic menu that not many regiments could furnish, a kind of weather that left nothing to be desired, and arrangements as nearly perfect and as nearly perfectly executed as human nature and circumstances would permit made this what our ever popular president termed it, "a *perfect excursion*."

And with this should be said a word for the splendid, magnanimous behavior of our people, men and women, old and young. No pleasanter, worthier grouping ever could be on such a trip. All conduct was unexceptionable. The ladies, so often the terror of such a trip, were to our excursion what the roses are to the garland, its beauty and sweetness, its choicest charm. Their courage, cheerfulness, thorough interest and unvarying good nature, have led us to say, verily, there never were any other ladies like the ladies of the Fourteenth Connecticut excursion party. God bless them!

67. Morton's Ford of the Rapidan seen from north bank.—Buckner House on hill towards left background.—Road opening just over head of Island.

STONY MOUNTAIN AND MORTON'S FORD.

ONE side trip, made by a few of the party, must, in the judgment of some, be written up: a trip to Stony Mountain and Morton's Ford, Va.—and that involves the rendering of the battle at the latter place.

No other winter camp of the Fourteenth has been so pleasantly remembered as that at Stony Mountain from Dec. 27, 1863, to May 3, 1864, and no battle was to the regiment what the battle of Morton's Ford was; for while this was not one of the great battles of the war the Fourteenth may be said to have been "in it" in the fullest sense.

The regiment had just completed some stylish and comfortable quarters near Stevensburg, Va., after the return from the Mine Run campaign, when, on Dec. 27, 1863, orders came for the brigade to march. Neither the pouring rain nor the men's hot anger could induce a modification of the order to go. The move was southward a few miles to a little elongated hill covered with pines and huge boulders, about one and one-half miles from Morton's Ford of the Rapidan. Here the men were told to build again, as they should stay all winter. The outlook was dreary, the land forbidding and the rain copious and cold. In a day or two, however, the weather was bright, and the soldiers, who had learned to make the best of everything, went earnestly to work and soon had, with their brigade, completed one of the best arranged, most convenient and attractive camps campaigners ever had. They've called

Brig. Camp, Stony Mountain, winter of 1864.—14th C. V. camp in foreground.

From drawing by Geo. W. Hill, of Co. G.

it their "Model Camp." Timber abounded, and all the streets and platforms in front of the huts were corduroyed, and sundry embellishments added not obtainable theretofore. The mountain, so called, was about one mile in

69.—Pony Mountain from Stevensburg, Va.—Cedar Mountain in left background.

extent on its longest axis, and the Fourteenth's camp was located on the lower part of its north-west slope. The camp of the 12th N. J. adjoined it, that of the 108th N. Y. was next beyond, and that of the 1st Del. farthest away. The camp of the 10th N. Y. Battln. was at the opposite end of the hill. There was to the regiment an unusual and delightful sense of independence in this camp, inasmuch as the brigade had the special duty of picketing the river, within the cavalry vidette line, and was so far from the main body of the army that general orders were not wont to trouble it. When the camp was completed the wives of some of the officers came and spent several weeks with them there— the only time the Fourteenth ever knew this golden chance. As this camp and the battlefield near do not lie on the route of general travel our men have not visited them, and there has long been a strong desire felt by some to embrace the first feasible opportunity for doing so. Accordingly, on the afternoon of Sept. 21st, after our return from Fredericksburg, Colonels Moore and Broatch and the writer, with hearts more elated than we could express, took train from Washington for it.

A run of a few miles took us to a region bristling with war time reminiscences. Fairfax Junction was passed, and soon we shot over that stream once utterly insignificant in our country's history but suddenly, in the summer of 1861, heard of the world around—Bull Run. Then soon appeared, out upon the plain, some high red earthworks of the once mysterious Manassas; then Bristoe Station, scene of one of our sharpest little fights, Oct. 14, 1863. Catlett's Station and Bealton Station, well remembered as great depots of

The Old Ground.

army supplies, appeared on their broad plains, and then Warrenton Junction where we bivouacked the night of November 15, 1862, on our way to Fredericksburg, and touched again in the summer and fall of 1863. We crossed the Rappahannock where five times we had crossed it on pontoons in the fall of 1863, and then passed Brandy Station, location of our principal depot of supplies in the winter of 1863-64 and near which were the chief field hospitals of the army that winter—where our wounded of the Morton's Ford battle were cared for.

Culpepper, our objective point on the railroad, was reached at an early evening hour and a little time spent in looking about that singular old town, so mixed up with the vibrations of the two opposing armies in this part of Virginia during a large part of the war time. An early start the next day, with a good team, and we were soon under the shadow of Pony Mountain —prominent in all our views when campaigning in that part of the country— on our way to Stevensburg.

The day was a perfect one. Happy as school-boys out on a lark our spirits rose steadily. Stevensburg reached we turned southward, and after driving about three miles over a road rough enough to make saints talk saucy turned into a field and drove for the southern part of Stony Mountain. A little farther drive and we were on the old parade ground of the Fourteenth. Then we entered the woods, completely grown over the

70.
Stony Mountain Va., in 1892.—Camp of 14th C. V. in left background, Parade-ground in foreground.

hill left bare when the regiment moved away, and stood among the relics of the old camp, our hearts crying out in the great solitude for the comrades there associated in the days of long ago. Positions were easily determined, and the boulders that looked so lovely once as street settings or inside tent ornaments were there, but the corduroy and the things indicating streets had vanished. One fire-place composed of large stones, strongly suggestive of sizzling pork and steaming coffee, and various heaps indicating where chimneys had stood were found; also old boots, rusty cans, broken bottles—proving how fond the Fourteenth men were of *pickles*—and slashed canteens, destroyed upon breaking camp to prevent their use by the enemy. A little climbing took us to the top of the hill where a fine view in all directions was afforded. The prominent Clark's Mountain, Lee's place of observation, below the Rapidan was in sight, and so was the battlefield of Morton's Ford.

And why is not this a good point and place to introduce the story of

THE BATTLE.

Early in February, 1864, it had been arranged by our highest military authorities that Genl. Butler should advance upon Richmond with a view to capture it. To divert the attention of Lee and make it appear necessary to hold his army intact near the Rapidan a demonstration was ordered made by the Second Corps at Morton's Ford and a simultaneous one by the First Corps at Raccoon Ford, about three miles above. Evidently it was not intended that an engagement should be hazarded or that a great force should be thrown across the river. The First Corps did not cross, but some leaders in the Second Corps, moved by spirits that have their proper place, if anywhere, within iron bound casks, where they should forever stay, essayed more than was purposed—hence the great woes, unrequited, of our regiment; for no good whatever seems to have come from the trouble, suffering and loss of that battle-day.

The First Corps, Genl. Newton, moved on the morning of Feb. 6 to the vicinity of Raccoon Ford, where it spent that day and the next in practical inactivity, returning to camp at dusk of the 7th. Genl. Warren, commanding the Second Corps, reports that orders were issued the night of the 5th to move the whole corps at daylight. Accordingly, early the next morning all the divisions of the Second Corps were headed towards Morton's Ford. At about 7 o'clock the Fourteenth, under command of Lieut. Col. S. A. Moore, with its brigade, commanded that day by Col. Powers of the 108th N. Y., left the snug quarters at Stony Mountain, having a good supply of ammunition and three days' rations, and, falling in behind the other brigades of the division coming from their camps back with the main army, moved through a belt of woods in front of the camp and turned towards the ford. This ford, one of the few passable places of this deep, swift stream, is about midway of a rectangular bend of the Rapidan whose convex side is northward and somewhat more than a mile long. A road approaches the river on each side obliquely from above. The head of an island appears between the debouchures of these roads, and at this point the stream broadens. The enemy had earthworks for artillery on the heights, more than a mile back from the ford, curv-

MORTON'S FORD—THE FIRST CROSSING.

ing towards the river at the extremes of the bend referred to. Also, they had a rifle-pit, containing about eighty men, beyond the river bank. Below the ford the public road runs, in a general direction, southward over a hill seen near the right of cut 67, and upon it, nearly one mile from the river, was the residence of Dr. Morton—not visible at the ford. About half way from the ford to this house a farm road enters said road on the left coming from the house of Major Buckner. The ford is reached from the Stevensburg highway by a farm road of over one-half mile length passing the Robinson house. Upon the plateau south-west of this house the artillery of the Second Corps was drawn up and near it much of the infantry. These were in plain sight of the enemy, the artillery being within range of his works. The lead of this movement, as well as nearly all the fighting, was to devolve on the Third Division, though the Second Division, Genl. Webb, was, later in the day, ordered over in support, to guard against a possible grand push of the enemy. Genl. Webb commanded the corps the most of the day, Genl. Warren pleading indisposition and not appearing on the field until late in the afternoon.

71.
Morton's Ford from south bank.—Head of Island in River seen.—Figure stands in Road.

At about 10.30 A. M. the Third Brig., Genl. Owen, of our Div., was ordered to effect a crossing, which it promptly proceeded to do. No provision had been made for bridging the stream, so real *fording* must be done. Three hundred selected veterans of the brigade were advanced as skirmishers, under command of Capt. Seabury. These quickly waded the stream, dashed up the bank, the brigade following, and charged the rifle-pits, capturing about thirty men. The enemy's batteries began playing upon them at once, and there was a quick run for the slope in front. Over the ridge the skirmishers and the brigade pushed, driving what of the enemy's infantry opposed them, and formed a line of skirmishers beyond the Morton house, (see cut 73) extending it through the fields at the left and to the rear of the Buckner premises. Immediately thereupon the enemy advanced a strong skirmish line in opposition, and at 12.30 o'clock Genl. Owen, as he says, seeing a heavy column of infantry moving into position towards his left sent request for reinforcements. At once the First Brig., Genl. Carroll, was sent over, arriving on the ground at 1.15. The force in front was steadily increasing, and as large masses of troops were seen moving from the direction of Clark's Mountain the call was soon made for additional reinforcements. Then our own brigade was ordered over. Genl. Owen says that this brigade reported at 2.15 P. M.

It was a rough thing to be obliged to wade a rapid stream, waist deep, when in midwinter water of melted snow and ice was flowing, and that in the midst of a drizzling rain that chilled to the bone and where the sand and ooze of the river-bed filled shoe and boot. But the Fourteenth did it, and moved quickly on up the slope towards the Buckner ridge. The enemy shelled briskly but no one of the regiment was hurt. Moving to rear of the Buckner house the regiment rested, with the brigade, awaiting orders. It was a most uncomfortable time. The clothing of the men was saturated with the icy water of the river and their shoes had not been cleared of its sand. The ground where they rested was wet and muddy and the disagreeable drizzle continued. While they were lying there, occasionally receiving a shelling, the skirmishers at the front were having a lively time, the enemy accumulating numbers and extending lines towards the river as though purposing a move to get between that and our forces. Pressing our line harder and harder, toward evening they made a vigorous attack and drove it back from its position beyond the Morton house towards the Buckner place and continued advancing. There was need of immediate action, for it looked as though an attack in force was contemplated. The 39th N. Y., the old "Garibaldi Guards," was ordered to advance and stop the enemy. This regiment being largely composed of new recruits, and those of a foreign tongue, totally unfit to be sent out for such a purpose at such a time and place, recoiled and was soon driven back in disorder. Something effective must be done instanter, and, passing over those who would have the preference, or obligation, in order, the commanding general called for his "Connecticut Yankees, who could be relied on." Col. Moore's voice, shrilly calling: "Forward, Fourteenth!" was heard, and without delay the men, stepping over the 12th N. J. men lying in their front, advanced to the ridge on which the Buckner house is located, deployed as skirmishers with short intervals of three or four feet. On passing over the ridge the line was exposed to a very hot fire of musketry from the rebel line advanced some distance in front of the Morton house and along the ridge at left and right of it. This galling fire made some of the recruits nervous, especially as now darkness had come on to that degree

FIGHTING IN THE DARK.   103

that the enemy's position could be seen but dimly, and a score or two were quite demoralized for a little time. But the officers promptly disciplined them and brought them to their places and their senses, and the sturdy old boys carried them right along. Adjutant Hincks, fearing an attempt to flank at the left by forces from the entrenchments on the hill, took a line to the left and held it rigidly there. Advancing down the slope and through the swale the regiment was subjected to a fire hotter and hotter, but courage and determination grew with every step and there was no faltering. When about one-half way across the swale Maj. Coit was struck, and left the field. Col. Moore, always cool of head and undaunted, and yet impetuous and almost fierce in a fight, rode along the line incessantly, his fine, penetrating voice ringing out orders in the increasing darkness, rallying the men and keeping them to their places and duty. The enemy stubbornly held position until the regiment reached the road. Here was a steep bank eight or ten feet high, (near third tree from right seen in cut 73) up which the men clambered, receiving a volley at the top. Col. Moore, being mounted, was obliged to ride up the

72.
Buckner House and Ridge seen from the Morton House Slope and Swale the 14th C. V. advanced over firing, Battle Morton's Ford.—Road fence in foreground at left.

road toward the house and the control of the right practically devolved on the commander of Co. A, Capt. Broatch. It was pitchy dark by this time and men could not see each other when a few feet apart. Only by the voices could they know where their commanders were, and only by the gun-flashes could one determine where his enemy was. As a command was given a volley was sent in that direction, and as a gun flashed it furnished a point to aim at. Almost the first order given after gaining the top of the bank drew a volley that took off one of Capt. Broatch's fingers and spoiled his sword-hilt and struck several men of his company and of Cos. D and F. The captain pushed forward holding his sword in his left hand, still guiding his men with his voice, when a shot cut his trusty blade in two, and his wound becoming very painful he was obliged to retire from the field. But the line was well under headway driving the rebel line back towards the house. It was a hand to hand fight in the inky darkness, the contending parties being but a few yards or feet apart.

That is a thrilling and desperate moment when men see their antagonists, a few steps away, only by the light coming from their gun muzzles and hear the whizz of the bullets or feel their blow almost simultaneously with seeing the flash. Such was it with the Fourteenth at this hour. Men were falling all the time; but they were winning and the end was nearing. When the regiment reached the Morton house the rebel force was massing behind it and among the outbuildings. Capt. Doten of Co. F went into the house with a

73.
Morton House seen from the Buckner House.—Scene of last struggle, Battle of Morton's Ford, Feb. 6, 1864.—Swale over which the 14th C. V. advanced.

few of his men. He could see that it would be madness to charge the enemy at the back of the house with his handful of men; but this very madness was required of him. The division commander came dashing up to the house, and entering in hot haste he demanded what the men were doing there. Capt. Doten attempted to explain the situation to him, but the general would listen to nothing, ordering, with many highly seasoned expressions after his usual style, an "immediate move out and on." There was nothing for the captain to do but to collect his men, open the back door of the house and step out. He straightway found himself confronted by eight companies of the 44th Georgia regiment, who mercifully refrained from firing at the party, saying it would be murder, as they had heard all the words uttered in the house. Of course there was an immediate demand for surrender and an immediate compliance—and that is how one of our most popular and gallant officers instead of going back to camp with his comrades that night spent the hours lonely and homesick at a smoldering fire among strangers and hostiles and the next day began his tedious midwinter trip to Libby. His captors assured him that they killed the officer on the white horse (Genl. Hays) for they saw him fall from his horse. The general was not killed, though he fell from his horse, and there was said to be a bullet hole in his saddle. He escaped in the darkness.

The Fourteenth had done its work, splendidly, grandly, driving back steadily a strong force at a most unfavorable hour and place and losing scores of men; but help was needed and the 108th N. Y. and the 10th N. Y. were ordered up quickly. The line was extended to the right by the 12th N. J. and other troops to foil the attempt at flanking, and soon the enemy was wholly routed and the fighting at an end.

Most of the regiments were sent over the river that evening, recrossing on a rough temporary foot-bridge built during the afternoon. Capt. Dewey of the 10th N. Y. reports that he "crossed about an hour after the last of the division crossed and rejoined his brigade early the next morning." The Fourteenth recrossed about 11 o'clock, bearing their many dead and wounded, and reached camp at midnight. Scarcely had the worn-out men betaken themselves to their bunks when an order came directing Col. Moore to take the regiment out and picket the river opposite the ford. This was a cruel order, for it was wholly unnecessary. Other troops there were that had done no hard duty that day; and there were none others that had done, considering the fighting and losses, as severe duty as the Fourteenth. There was no release, however, and the regiment turned out at once and marched back to the river, not being relieved and allowed to return to camp until noon of the 8th.

Who will deny that the Fourteenth men had hard fare? But these things have made their record—their pride to-day. While the action was waging during daylight the ladies in camp witnessed from the top of Stony Mountain, with what solicitude no tongue can describe, the struggle involving the lives of their husbands and friends; and as the night contest raged in the blackness they saw the lines of fire, like the fitful, fierce lightning's play, from mouths of speaking muskets with an agony of soul unutterable.

FIGURES THAT TELL—AN UNJUST CHARGE.

Official Report of Casualties, Battle of Morton's Ford, Va., February 6, 1864.

	Killed.	Wounded.	Captured and Missing.	Aggregate.
Second Army Corps	11	203	40	254
3d Division of 2d A. C.	11	201	40	252
2d Brig., 3d Div., 2d A. C.	7	116	23	146
2d Brig., 3d Div., 2d A. C., by Regiments:				
14th Conn	6	90	19	115
12th N. J.		11	....	11
1st Del		6	4	10
108th N. Y.		7	....	7
10th N. Y.	1	2	....	3
	Killed and mortally wounded.			
Corrected Report of 14th Conn	14	85	16	115

The above figures tell the Fourteenth's story eloquently and adequately. With them before us the writer feels compelled to here touch upon one subject for the honor of the dear old regiment, for his heart is hot within him at every thought of it.

In the division commander's official report of the Morton's Ford affair, a report by no means commensurate with the importance and details of it, occurs this passage: "I regret to forward such a long list of casualties, but it is solely attributable to the faltering of two regiments of conscripts or substitutes comprising the Fourteenth Connecticut and Thirty-ninth New York Volunteers." It will be observed in the above quotation that the commander makes his explanatory statement to account for "such a long list of casualties," which he "regrets to forward," and that he places the Fourteenth Connecticut *first* in naming the faulty regiments. Of the 39th N. Y. men we may not properly, perhaps, speak, though our belief is that the remark quoted is unjust as regarding them, and that the fault was not so much theirs as of the commander who ordered them in; but of the Fourteenth we unhesitatingly pronounce it unjust, cruel, and untrue, and if there is not a dash of malice in it the writer is misimpressed. Possibly Genl. Hays' own pen did not indite it, but it was given as his report and must so remain always. Our brigade commander mentions with strong commendation the conduct of the Fourteenth and the actions of its officers, and has not a suggestion of criticism of either. The division commander gave not the slightest recognition of the good conduct or hard fare of the regiment, nor did he recommend any of its officers for promotion, while he did highly extol the commander of a regiment of the First Brigade, whose total casualties were eleven wounded.

The Fourteenth was not a "regiment of conscripts or substitutes." Though a large number of these had been added to the organization during the preceding seven months, most of them had received a good seasoning in the campaigns of the fall and the battle of Bristoe Station in October and in the Mine Run campaign in November and December, and they had performed guard, picket, and drill duty with the veterans all through the season. The backbone of the regiment was the old, well tried, reliable, original material, officers and men, and when some of the new men hesitated, as was natural, at the severely trying ordeal at the beginning of the advance into action the veterans threw around them the cords of their influence and bound them fast to the line, and all went on together. When men would advance steadily nearly one-half mile under the conditions heretofore described, in the darkness, guided only by the light of the musket discharges right in their faces, against a strong line of veteran braves well located and drive them to cover and not retire until their work was fully done, when one had only to drop down in the line as though bullet struck and then as the line swept on in the darkness rise and slip to the rear unobserved, such could not be called cowards or falterers. Computations based on latest data show that of the fourteen of our regiment killed or mortally wounded at the battle eight were recruits; that of the wounded forty-nine were, and of the captured thirteen, seven of whom died in rebel prisons (practically killed by that engagement), making *seventy* casualties of *recruits*, or two-thirds of all the regiment's casualties. And these fell *all along* the course from the start to the finish. Does this showing indicate that the new men were falterers? Major Hincks fitly wrote: "Men do not stand still and allow themselves to be shot down until one-third of their number have fallen. If they (the Fourteenth) had been terrified or panic-struck as is represented, they would have retreated in disorder instead of advancing towards the quarter from which the fire came." Genl. Hays' subsequent solicitude concerning the condition of these men, visiting the hospitals and making careful inquiries as to their progress and causing delicacies to be supplied them, evinced that he, as says Maj. Hincks, did not regard them "a parcel of cowards who owe their injuries solely to their bad behavior." It is evident that his conscience troubled him—and well it might. Brave as he was, and he taught our men helpful lessons in daring individual exposure, the spirit of "John Barleycorn," that hurtful foe of our army, and indeed of both armies, ruled him when it should not. It ruled him on the afternoon and evening of Feb. 6, 1864, as it ruled more than one other commander of troops in the Second Corps that day, making him reckless and passionate and blind; and brave and devoted officers and men, whose lives were precious, suffered the grievous results.

Of the fact stated the Fourteenth men generally were well aware, and Capt. W. H. Hawley of the regiment, that day on the brigade staff, a man of intelligence, veracity, kind-heartedness and courage unimpeachable, has left a record from his pen stating this as "a solemn fact," emphatically saying: "It is the truth." That inimical, cruel charge, made to excuse the fatal results of an action that the higher powers evidently had not intended should be hazarded, stands against our noble regiment, and in the public archives and their published reproductions it must stand forever; how improperly and unjustly let the readers of these pages judge. Thus have we written that facts may be set forth and our regiment exonerated while some of us live who have facilities and temper for doing it.

Now to our trip and our trio. We tarried on the mountain as long as would do, filled with sunshine as was the earth about us, and then reluctantly left it to make our way to the ford. We stopped at the Robinson house near the ford, familiar to all our men as headquarters of the picket. B. recalled the stormy nights when, returning from the "rounds," he and others had been allowed by the kindly old couple living here to lie on the floor by a rousing fire, and that the good people had cooked for them their coffee and "rations," glad to themselves have a treat of the things then rare luxuries to them. Soon we were chatting with a comely matron who, surrounded by her children, was working in the shade at rear of the house. She had funds of information of the kind we desired. She remembered the Fourteenth

Robinson House near Morton's Ford, north side.—Headquarters of picket.

Connecticut well, and said she was the Lucy Brown who used to come with her sister Betty Brown to the dances the Fourteenth had, when all the available ladies in the vicinity were invited. She mentioned our band and many incidents that proved her knowledge of the things talked of; and she gave information solicited regarding certain persons known to our party, particularly of one rosy damsel Susie whose rustic charms had seriously "Hitt" some of our bachelor officers.

From this place we went to the ford, driving across with the water deep to the wagon body. Going over the hill toward the Morton house we turned to the left and stopped to make inquiries at a house prominent in view on the hill. A man of elderly appearance and stately mien approached the gate to speak to us. He was the proprietor of the place and announced himself to us as Major Calhoun C. Buckner. He pressed us to enter his grounds and prolong our stay. He was cordial, affable, courteous and intelligent,

A Noble Host and Happy Hours.

awakening our interest in him at once. When introduced to each of us in turn and told who we were, he seemed to enjoy the surprise given him, and he said, with a merry twinkle of his eyes: "I should know you were not *southern* gentlemen, for if you were a *bottle* would have been in sight before this." He told us that he was in the Confederate service during most of the war. He said that when he "got through the service he was thankful that he had got through alive and felt that he had had enough of war;" that he was "like the man who made a bargain with the devil, that if he would leave him alone he would let him alone," and that he had "not been to a military meeting or a monument unveiling since." He was surprised to learn from us how serious an engagement had taken place on his premises in February, 1864, having scarcely heard of it before. He regaled us with many witty stories and legends of the war days and devoted himself assiduously to our entertainment, urging that we spend days with him. Failing to induce us to be his guests at table, he insisted on adding, on behalf of himself and his wife, sundry improvements to our lunch set out on his porch, such as conserves and relishes, and pitchers of milk and new cider, partaking with us somewhat for hospitality's sake. So, with such pleasurable

75.   "Island View," Major Buckner's House.

sociability, resting on the grass in the shade, soldier fashion, looking over the battlefield and contrasting its appearance with that it bore on a certain chill and bloody day nearly twenty-eight years before, the halcyon hours of this unmatched day sped on until we saw that we must begone. Now our warm-hearted host, loth to have us leave him, hunted up an excuse to detain us, and finding and bringing on some melons, we must, forsooth, stay until these had been well discussed. When we in earnest started to leave, the Major accompanied us to his gate, showing signs of real regret at our departure. Then we went towards the Morton house, clambering up the bank where the right of the regiment went up at the time of the battle and approaching it as the regiment did. We found the barn and other out-buildings apparently unchanged, but the original dwelling house had burned down a few years ago and a brick building had been erected on its site. This last spot of thrilling interest visited, we started for home, crossing the river at Raccoon Ford, now provided with a good iron bridge, and then drove over ten miles to Culpeper. Tired we were, and a little sore with the jolting and shaking, but happy all through, chatting, singing old melodies and gazing at the country.

One year later, the same party minus Col. Moore but plus Maj. Hincks, Sergts. Hirst and Blatchley and the son of the latter, made nearly the same trip, reaching Culpeper on a Saturday night on our way back from a trip to Richmond and Petersburg, where we had visited forts "Steadman," "Hell," "Morton," the "Crater," Ream's Station, etc. Sunday was almost a precise reprint of the day of our trip in 1891. On the top of Stony Mountain

76. "Coffee ready!" Old Fire-Place, Camp 14th C. V., Stony Mountain, Va.

at noon, on a great rock platform with a huge boulder pulpit, we had a little service of devotion, singing and talk, that will never be forgotten by the participants. The day—

"so cool, so calm, so bright,
The bridal of the earth and sky,"

the place, the memories, the comradeship made it an hour whose treasuring we hope eternity will not rob us of. Our kodakist essayed to pepetuate for us, and for this volume, the place and group, but it was too good to keep thus—the film broke down under the effulgence and joy.

We drove to the Robinson house and then crossed the ford, Mr. James Nalle, the present proprietor and occupant of the Robinson place, courteously, and voluntarily, riding ahead and guiding us. Our friend Major Buckner recognized some of us instantly and took us all right into his warm heart. This time he and his excellent wife compelled our participation at their bountiful table, and then he devoted himself to our pleasure. Another delightful afternoon upon the lawn in pleasant converse and viewing the old field; the same old tactics of the major to prolong our stay; then an adjournment to the large hall of the mansion to sing at the organ with the major's comely daughters and their young lady chum, when "Nearer my God to thee" and "Praise God from whom all blessings flow" came from grateful hearts over earnest lips; then a hurried hand-shaking and a fervid good-bye, while of our group every eye was dewy, every soul tender and every heart saying "Grace, mercy and peace be with you," and we tore ourselves away from our noble host and his charming family and turned homeward, stopping a little time at the Morton house on our way. Such a day cannot be effaced from memory, nor should it be. Our only regret was that every good man of the old Fourteenth could not share our privilege and our happiness. That they may know of them this is written.

CORRECTIONS.

Page 11, fourth line; for "see in cut 14" read see cut 12.
Page 53, eighteenth line; for "cuts 28 and 30" read cuts 24 and 28.

LIST OF ENGAGEMENTS

OF THE 14TH C. V.

BATTLES.

Antietam, Md.,	September 17, 1862.
Fredericksburg, Va.,	December 12, 13, 14, "
Chancellorsville, Va.,	May 2 and 3, 1863.
Gettysburg, Pa.,	July 2, 3, 4, "
Bristoe Station, Va.,	October 14, "
Morton's Ford, Va.,	February 6, 1864.
Wilderness (Todd's Tavern), Va.,	May 5, "
Wilderness, Va.,	May 6, "
Laurel Hill, Va.,	May 10, "
Spottsylvania, Va.,	May 12, "
North Anna River, Va.,	May 24, "
Tolopotomy, Va.,	May 30, "
Cold Harbor, Va.,	June 3, "
Cold Habor, Va.,	June 5, "
Petersburg, Va.,	June 17, "
Ream's Station, Va.,	August 25, "

MINOR ENGAGEMENTS AND SKIRMISHES.

Falling Waters, Md.,	July 14, 1863.
Auburn, Va.,	October 14, "
Blackburn's Ford, Va.,	October 15, "
Mine Run, Va.,	November 30, "
Spottsylvania, Va.,	May 13, 1864.
Spottsylvania, Va.,	May 14, "
Spottsylvania, Va.,	May 18, "
Milford Station, Va.,	May 22, "
North Anna River, Va.,	May 26, "
Petersburg, Va.,	June 16, "
Deep Bottom, Va.,	August 15, "
Deep Bottom, Va.,	August 16, "
Hatcher's Run (Boydton Plank Road), Va.,	October 27, "
Hatcher's Run, Va.,	February 5, 1865.
Hatcher's Run, Va.,	March 29, "
High Bridge, Va.,	} March 30, "
Farmville, Va.,	to
Surrender of Lee's Army, Appomattox C. H, Va.,	April 10. "

THE EXCURSIONISTS.*

Adams, James K., ... Seymour, Conn.
Adams, William A., ... " "
Allen, Mrs. R., ... Meriden, "
Alling, C. D., Mr. and Mrs., . Waterbury, "
†*Andrews, T. D.*, . . . " "
Andrews, Miss Bessie, . . . New Britain, Conn.
Andross, W. W., Mr. and Mrs., . Rockville, "
Bailey, N. S, Mr. and Mrs., . . Buckingham, "
Barber, Samuel, ... Jewett City, "
Barnes, Charles D., Mr. and Mrs., Southington, "
Bart, Henry N., ... New York, N. Y.
Bartholomew, T. L., . . Bridgeport, Conn.
Bartlett, E. S., ... Hartford, "
Bartlett, F. W., . . " "
Beach, Henry A., ... New Britain, "
Beam, Alfred A., Mr. and Mrs., . " " "
Beam, Charles, . . . " " "
Beaton, C. H., Mr. and Mrs., . " " "
Beaton, Miss Minnie L., . . " " "
Billings, W. H., . . . Somersville, "
Blakeslee, Ralph N., Mr. and Mrs.. . . Waterbury, "
Blatchley, Charles G., . . Philadelphia, Pa.
Blatchley, Charles H., . " "
Bosworth, N. A., . . . Hartford, Conn.
Boughton, G. A., ... Waterbury, "
Brigham, George N., . . Rockville, "
Broatch, John C., Mr. and Mrs., . Middletown, Conn.
Broatch, J. Allison, . . " "
Broatch, Robert, . . " "
Brooks, Henry S., . . . " "
Bullard, Henry, . . " "
Bunce, James H., Mr. and Mrs., . " "
Burke, Robert. Mr. and Mrs., . " "
Bunnell, Charles R., Mr. and Mrs , Bristol, "
Calvert, J. C., ... New London, "
Carpenter, H. E., . . East Hampton, "
Carroll, W. N., . . . Yalesville, "
Chapman, Mrs. M. J. H., . Middletown, "
Charter, Irving W., . . . East Haddam, "
Chatfield, John D., . Waterville, "
Clarke, H. L., ... East Hampton, "

* This list is as nearly accurate as we have been able to make it. Some names may be here that should not be and some may not be that should be. Several persons were booked who failed to appear, and some joined the party who did not report their names. We have obtained most of the latter through correspondence. The R.R. Co. reports three hundred tickets sold at Jersey City, and eleven persons joined us at other points.
† Names appearing in *italics* are those of members of the Fourteenth.

Clark, E. R., ... Hartford, Conn.
Coffin, O. V., Hon. and Mrs., . . Middletown, Conn.
Coit, James B., . . . Washington, D. C.
Colby, E. C., . . . Waterbury, Conn.
Colgrove, Mrs. A. M., . . Middletown, "
Colgrove, Miss Mary S., . " "
Colgrove, Miss Adelaide W., " "
Condon, J. C., ... Springfield, Mass.
Cooley, Henry M., Mr. and Mrs., " "
Cornwell, J. C., . . . Hartford, Conn.
Cowles, Alfred, . " "
Crawford, F. M., . . . New Haven, "
Crittenden, A. R., Mr. and Mrs., Middletown, Conn.
Curtis, J. P., . . . New Britain, "
Davis, Samuel H., . . New York, N. Y.
Davis, D. Newland, . . Middletown, Conn.
Davis, L. O., Mr. and Mrs., " "
Dean, William H., . . Letcher, South Dakota.
Denio, L. F., Mr. and Mrs., Middletown, Conn.
Dennison, George E., . Hartford, "
Dorman, W. B., . . . Newington, "
Dorman, Lewis W., . . " "
Dowd, Frank C., . Madison, "
Dwinell, S. O., . . Birmingham, "
Easton, Walter R., . . . Meriden, "
Edwards, Watson, Mr. and Mrs., . Portland, "
Elliott, Joseph T., Mr. and Mrs., Middletown, "
Farley, Fred. A., . . . Pine Meadow, "
Farnham, Edwin D., . Vinton Mills, "
Ferguson, James F., . . Waterbury, "
Finn, Thomas, . . . Birmingham, Conn.
Fiske, Wilbur D., Mr. and Mrs., . Boston, Mass.
Fitzpatrick, John J., . . New Haven, Conn.
Fletcher, Charles, Mr. and Mrs , . Emporia, Kansas.
Flood, Andrew, . . East Hampton, Conn.
Forbes, William, . . . Lawrence, Mass.
Fox, Hiram H., Mr. and Mrs., New Haven, Conn.
Francis, F. H., . " " "
Franklin, L. W., . . . Manchester, "
Gallup, Rev. James A., . Madison, "
Gardner, Thomas W., . . New London, "
Geer, Everett S., . . Hartford, "
Gibbons, Fred E., . Middletown, "
Gibbud, D D., . . . Naugatuck, "
Gladden, Miss C. N., . Portland, "
Glenn, Russell, . . Bridgeport, "
Goldsmith, Mrs. O. C., New Haven, "
Goodman, Edward, . Birmingham, "
Goodrich, Loren H., . Burnside, "
Gould, John M., . Portland, Me.
Gould, Oliver C., . " "
Griswold, H., . . . Hartford, Conn.
Griswold, Walter B., " "
Grumley, William R., . Meriden, "
Guild, Augustus, . . Middletown, "

THE EXCURSIONISTS.

Guilford, William O.,	Waterbury, Conn.
Gurnan, Andrew,	" "
Hahn, Joseph,	" "
Hall, George,	" "
Hall, William H.,	Middletown, "
Hall, Albert F., Mr. and Mrs.,	Meriden, "
Hall, John M.,	Madison, "
Hammond, A. Park, Mr. and Mrs.,	Rockville, "
Hammond, Allyn,	" "
Harris, George H., Mr. and Mrs.,	Middletown, "
Hart, William W.,	Philadelphia, Pa.
Hart, M. R.,	Naugatuck, Conn.
Henn, George F.,	New Britain, "
Higby, F. A.,	Meriden, "
Hill, Thomas M.,	Waterbury, "
Hirst, Benjamin,	Springfield, Mass.
Hirst, John.	Rockville, Conn.
Hogan, Thomas,	Birmingham, "
Holley, James, Mr. and Mrs.,	New Britain, "
Howard, A. E.,	Hartford, "
Howell, Edwin A.,	New Haven, "
Hubbard, J. M.,	Middletown, "
Hubbard, Mrs. J. W.,	" "
Hubbard, Miss M. Louise,	" "
Hubbard, George A.,	Washington, D. C.
Hubbard, L. V. B.,	Birmingham, Conn.
Hunn, George A., Mr. and Mrs.,	New Britain, "
Hyde, Elbert F., Mr. and Mrs.,	Ellington. "
Inglis, James, Mr. and Mrs.,	Middletown, "
Jewett, Levi, Dr. and Mrs.,	Cobalt, "
Jordan, William P.,	Portland, Me.
Kamak, I. H.,	Waterbury, Conn.
Kincaid, John,	Middletown, "
Knowlton, Julius W., Mr. and Mrs.,	Bridgeport, "
Kurtz, George,	Chicago, Ill.
Lane, J. W.,	Wallingford, Conn.
Lane, W. F.,	" "
Latimer, William R.,	Bloomfield, "
Latimer, Miss Edith E.,	" "
Leach, C. B., Mr. and Mrs.,	Middletown, "
Lillibridge, George H.,	Washington, D. C.
Lines, John, Mr. and Mrs.,	Waterbury, Conn.
Little, Elmer,	Birmingham, "
Lydall, Henry, Mr. and Mrs.,	Manchester, "
Lyman, Miss Emma E.,	Willimantic. "
Lyman, Charles,	Washington, D. C.
McCarthy, Miss Emma,	Waterbury, Conn.
McCarthy, Miss Mary C.,	
McPherson, John,	Rockville, "
McVey, John, Rev. and Mrs.,	Manchester, "
Meigs, Hon. James R.,	Madison, "
Meigs, John H.,	" "
Merwin, R. T., Mr. and Mrs.,	New Haven, "
Metcalf, F. E.,	Rockville, "
Metcalf, W. A.,	" "
Miles, Hon. W. A.,	Meriden, "

THE EXCURSIONISTS.

Minor, Mrs. Charles H.,	Boston, Mass.
Mohr, Henry,	Canarsie, N. Y.
Moody, Edgar,	East River, Conn.
Moore, Samuel A., Mr. and Mrs.,	New Britain, "
Moore, Miss Roberta,	" " "
Moore, Mrs. C. H.,	" " "
Murdock, Thomas,	Middletown, "
Murdock, John M.,	Portland, "
Neale, E. J., Mr. and Mrs.,	Southington, "
Newton, H. F.,	Plainfield, "
Nichols, S. V., Mr. and Mrs.,	Bridgeport, "
Nichols, William B.,	" "
Norton, Charles W., Mr. and Mrs.,	New Britain, "
Norton, Master Dan.,	" " "
Norton, George S., Mr. and Mrs.,	New Haven, "
O'Connell, Michael, Mr. and Mrs.,	New Britain, "
O'Leary, Patrick,	Putnam, "
Palmer, John G.,	Middletown, "
Palmer, Miss Emma G.,	" "
Park, Chauncey T.,	New Britain, "
Parker, Hiland H.,	Chicago, Ill.
Parkhurst, B. B., Mr. and Mrs.,	New Haven, Conn.
Peck, B. A.,	Naugatuck, "
Pelton, James P.,	Portland, "
Pierce, Ernest C.,	New Britain, "
Porter, Ira A.,	" " "
Pratt, Thomas S., Mr. and Mrs.,	Rockville, "
Price, Robert C.,	Hartford, "
Prior, I. B.,	Cromwell, "
Pritchard, W. L. G.,	West Haven, "
Quirk, Michael J,	New Britain, "
Ray, George H., Mr. and Mrs.,	Florence, Mass.
Redfield, Charles H.,	Madison, Conn.
Roberts, J. T.,	Waterbury, "
Robinson, David W.,	Durham, "
Rossberg, C. C.,	New Britain, "
Russell, Charles A., Hon. and Mrs.,	Killingly, "
Sanford, Mrs. C. C.,	Bridgeport, "
Sargent, Mrs. Alice W.,	Boston, Mass.
Schmidt, J. W., Mr. and Mrs.,	New Britain, Conn.
Schlichter, Joseph,	Middletown, "
Seinsoth, J. J.,	Hartford, "
Scranton, J. S.,	Madison, "
Seward, Samuel H., Mr. and Mrs.,	Putnam, "
Sherman, Ernest,	Middletown, "
Simmons, W. S., Hon. and Mrs.,	Central Village, Conn.
Simmons, Miss Agnes L.,	" " "
Sprague, Mrs. Julia M.,	" " "
Smith, William D.,	Middletown, "
Smith, Friend H., Mr. and Mrs.,	Whigville, "
Smith, Edward,	Norfolk, "
Smith, Miss Annie,	Willimantic, "
Snagg, Reuben G., Mr. and Mrs.,	Waterbury, "
Snell, Samuel, Mr. and Mrs.,	Holyoke, Mass.
Southmayd, George M.,	Middletown, Conn.
Spencer, Imri A.,	Waterbury, "

The Excursionists.

Stannard, Miss Emma,	Southington, Conn.
Stedman, D. R.,	Rockville, "
Stevens, Henry S.,	Washington, D. C.
Stevens, O. H.,	Waterbury, Conn.
Stocking, George A.,	Wallingford "
Stowe, Nathan E., Mr. and Mrs.,	Brooklyn, N. Y.
Stow, Miss Mary,	Southington, Conn.
Stroud, Edwin, Mr. and Mrs.,	Middletown, "
Swan, Horace,	Westerly, R. I.
Sweet, Dr. F. A.,	Manchester, Conn.
Thompson, Ralph S.,	Winthrop, "
Thrall, W. G.,	New Britain, "
Thomson, Frank L.,	Albany, N. Y.
Tift, J. M.,	Jewett City, Conn.
Tift, W. H.,	" " "
Tillinghast, A. H.,	Hartford, "
Tomlinson, Dr. Charles,	" "
Tomlinson, Oliver K.,	Bridgeport, "
Townsend, James L.,	Noroton, "
Tubbs, William H.,	New London, Conn.
Tryon, A. C.,	Meriden, "
Tyler, Elnathan B.,	" "
Tracy, Mrs. Mary,	Cobalt, "
Vensel, Charles N., Mr. and Mrs.,	New Haven, "
Vinton, Mrs. Ella M.,	New Britain, "
Vinton, C. C.,	Vinton Mills, "
Wade, Edward H.,	Northampton, Mass.
Waite, Otis H.,	Naugatuck, Conn.
Walker, Robert,	Hartford, "
Walker, Jerome W.,	Waterbury, "
Ward, William S., Mr. and Mrs.,	Southington, "
Warner, W. H., Mr. and Mrs.,	Manchester, "
Watson, Master Eddie S.,	Putnam, "
Wilcox, Benjamin C.,	Meriden, "
Wilcox, W. H.,	" "
Wilcox, A. N.,	Guilford, "
Williams, E. H., Mr. and Mrs.,	Hartford, "
Wilson, M. V.,	New York, N. Y.
Wolf, Robert,	Hartford, Conn.
Wood, S. H., Mr. and Mrs.,	New Britain, "
Wood, M. M.,	" " "
Woodworth, Frank,	New London, "
Worcester, George E.,	Glastonbury, "
Young, Robert C.,	Middletown, "
Zacker, Hon. Edward,	Madison, "

www.ingramcontent.com/pod-product-compliance
Lightning Source LLC
Chambersburg PA
CBHW020125170426
43199CB00009B/648